Fake Smiles

William P. Rogers with Tony, 1944

Fake Smiles

Tony Rogers

TIDEPOOL PRESS

Cambridge, Massachusetts

Published in the United States in 2017 by TidePool Press

TidePool Press
6 Maple Avenue, Cambridge, Massachusetts 02139
www.tidepoolpress.com

Printed in the United States

Library of Congress Cataloging-in-Publication Data

Rogers, Tony 1940-
    Fake Smiles
    p.cm.
    ISBN 978-0-9914523-2-3
    1. Rogers, Tony, Cambridge, Massachusetts—United States—
    Biography 2. Memoir 3. Politics—Washington, D.C. 4. Writing
    I. Title.

2016954985

To my parents

ADELE LANGSTON ROGERS
August 15, 1911-May 27, 2001

WILLIAM P. ROGERS
June 23, 1913-January 2, 2001

AUTHOR'S NOTE

Because of the passage of time, I have recreated some dialogue and altered some chronology.

CONTENTS

Fake Smiles

1968

AT THE DINNER TABLE. A few weeks after Nixon won the presidency.

"How could voters be so stupid?" I demanded. I was twenty-eight and passionately anti-Nixon, even though he and Dad were friends.

"Calm down," Dad said. "He's going to be president. There is nothing you can do about it."

"God help us."

"Wait and see. Dick may surprise you. He's worked his whole life for this and knows what's at stake."

"Will he offer you a position in his administration?" Richard Nixon was Dad's longtime political ally. Dad had been attorney general when Nixon was vice president. He and Nixon golfed together on weekends and often came to our house for a drink afterward.

"I doubt it."

"Why not? You work well together."

"He knows I'm happy practicing law."

"What if he does offer you a position?"

"I'll thank him very much and tell him I'm not interested."

Mother spoke from her end of the table, her voice a symphony of support. "You'd do such a good job for him, Bill."

"Adele, you know I don't want to be in government again."

"But you'd be great." *Great* was one of Mother's favorite words. She said it like Kellogg's Frosted Flakes Tony the Tiger, a cartoon character who split the word into two syllables and growled the first—*Grrrr-rate!*

Me and my big mouth. "Will Dean Rusk stay on as secretary of state? He's been terrible on the war. Does he honestly believe if we don't defeat the communists in Vietnam they'll land in San Diego?"

"I'm sure Dick will want someone new in that position."

I was a Harvard Law School graduate. I had practiced law on Wall Street for a year before moving to Paris, where I worked at a boys school and wrote bad fiction. I had just returned to the States married to a Spanish Basque woman I barely knew and was driving a cab to support my writing habit. I was writing in our Arlington, Virginia, apartment on Saturday morning when Dad called. His voice lacked the combative edge it often had with me. He skipped the preliminaries. "Tony, it's Dad."

"Hi, Dad."

"I hope you'll be gentler on me than you were on Dean Rusk, because I'm going to be the next secretary of state."

I was too stunned to think, then more thoughts ran through my mind than my brain could process. Dad will be working for a president I despise. Dad will be one of the people running a war I hate. What would this do to my relationship with him, which was already rocky?

"I don't know what to say. I'm in shock."

"Me too," he said.

"Did you know this was coming?"

"No. Dick's offer came out of the blue."

"Wow."

"Wish me luck."

"Of course. You'll be great."

"Thanks. I have to call your siblings now."

"Okay. Congratulations, Dad."

I hung up and stood by the window looking out at busy Lee Highway. Cars streamed by as if nothing had changed. I had trouble breathing.

I decided, then and there, that I would stay out of the Washington fishbowl as much as possible while still being supportive of Dad. When he was attorney general in the Eisenhower administration, I had gone through the usual teenage struggles of establishing an independent identity, which had been made harder by his position. Every time I argued with him—which I did frequently about almost everything—he held the trump card of not only being my father, but also being attorney general. Who was I to argue with the attorney general of the United States? Now he'd hold an even higher position, upping the ante. To Dad's credit, he never played the trump card. He didn't have to.

His appointment was announced on Wednesday. Headlines in the papers, leading story on the nightly news. My name and the names of my three siblings at the tail end of the print stories. "Sons and daughter of … ."

On the lighter side, I could safely bet I'd be the only cab driver whose father was secretary of state.

Nixon assumed office on January 20, 1969, and to my surprise the Republic did not fall, nor did I revert to the days I felt totally eclipsed by Dad. What did change was my access to the secretary of state. I could harangue him in his house, by his pool, in his limo.

CHAPTER ONE

Competition

WHEN I WAS NINE, our family moved to Bethesda, Maryland, so that Dad could become counsel to a Senate Investigating Committee, which is when he got to know a new member of the House of Representatives, Richard Nixon. Washington then was a sleepy Southern town with one industry, the federal government. *The Washington Post* covered government gossip the way *Variety* and *Billboard* covered entertainment gossip, the ins and outs of Washington insiders apparently being of utmost importance to the survival of the Republic. We moved into a three-story, four-bedroom house on three-quarters acre of land. The large front yard sloped down to winding Glenbrook Road. In the summer, when the heat and humidity rose and the trees were in full bloom, there was a languorous feeling on the street, an atmosphere of delicious asphyxiation, as if one couldn't get enough oxygen by breathing but would be perfectly fine as long as one didn't move.

Family roles were beginning to be set among us four children. The oldest, my sister Dale, was the doer and joiner of the family. I, the second child and oldest son, had been shy all my life and was showing signs of becoming a loner. Jeff, the second son, quiet and amiable, was unmolded clay. Doug, the youngest, was just plain nice. There was a nine-year age gap between Dale and Doug.

The Rogers children from a 1951 Christmas card
(left to right) *Doug, Jeff, Tony and Dale*

Dale and I lived across a hall from each other on the third floor. Jeff and Doug lived on the second floor, as did our parents. The family ate dinners together. Mother did the cooking, we kids the cleanup.

Three years after the family moved into the house, newly-elected President Dwight Eisenhower appointed my father deputy attorney general. It was business as usual that evening for the Rogers household. "Do we still have to do the clean up?" I mock groaned, drying a plate after dinner.

"Yes, dear," Mother said. A regal, black-haired woman with a high forehead, she never raised her voice, never swore. Her harshest words, reserved for those rare occasions when she was beside herself with rage, were "hell's bells."

"A maid doesn't come with the job?" I wasn't serious for a minute.

"Dummy," Jeff said. "Everyone knows that."

"He wasn't serious," Dale said.

"What's the use of being deputy attorney general if you don't get a maid?" I insisted.

William P. Rogers served as deputy attorney general from 1953-1957. In this photo Rogers is sworn in as attorney general on November 11, 1957 as the family looks on. (Left to right) *William P. Rogers, President Dwight D. Eisenhower, Chief Justice Earl Warren*

"Stop it," Dale said. "I know you're not serious."

I quit, but not without grumbling, "I *hate* drying dishes."

"We are very fortunate," Mother said to us. "We have a lovely house and Dad has a wonderful new job. We are much more fortunate than many. Be grateful."

"Can we at least get a dishwasher?"

"When it's not an extravagance. Now finish up and go do your homework."

We dried the last of the dishes, put them away and were about to disperse when Mother reminded us, "The photographer from *Parade* will be here tomorrow. Dress appropriately."

Our picture appeared a few weeks later on the cover of *Parade* magazine, the Sunday supplement which reached millions of newspaper readers in those days. Dad was a photogenic example of the young men Eisenhower was choosing for his administration. We stood in the front yard for the picture. The family hadn't yet perfected its posed smiles, but my father looked movie-star handsome, my mother tall and serene with a genuinely warm smile. Later, after the mailing list for the family Christmas card grew to number in the thousands and after we had been photographed for numerous magazines and newspapers, our posed smiles became perfected, and you couldn't tell the real from the fake. But at the time of the *Parade* cover, we were novices.

I received fan mail after the picture appeared. Eight letters, if I remember correctly. All from girls. Several enclosed their pictures. My favorite was from a girl two years older than me who wrote, "Your father is very handsome, but he is too old for me. You are closer to my age, so I will write you instead."

Competition outside the realms of sport and business can be an insidious thing. This is especially true when the competition is between father and son. If the son wins, it means the father is a loser. If the son loves the father, he doesn't want to do that to him. If, on the other hand, the father wins, the son feels like a loser. And since most sons want the approval of their fathers, this means a loving son is banished to the loser bin until he can figure out a way to break free without wounding his father.

"Do you want to play catch?" Dad asked me one sunny afternoon.

"I'd rather stay indoors."

"You've got to get outdoors. You need sun, you're too pale. Come on."

Useless to resist. We went outside to the front lawn. The sun was relentless. "Put your shoulder into it," Dad urged after I had lobbed a few balls.

He wasn't satisfied. He came over, gripped my wrist with one hand and swung my arm in a wide arc. "Get some oomph behind it."

He stepped back and nodded. "Let it fly." The ball was wildly off-target. "No, no! You'll never be good if you're that wild. Concentrate."

He retrieved the ball and tossed it back.

"Dad, I just want to have fun."

"You can't have fun at something unless you're good at it. Try again."

I tried and tried but soon got bored. If something bored me, I had a hard time concentrating. By the time we went indoors, Dad was thoroughly exasperated. "Don't you care? Don't you care? If you want to get ahead in life, you need to care."

I went up to my third floor room. I was sweating and uncomfortable, but the shower was on the second floor and I wanted to stay out of Dad's sight. I hated to take showers. Once I got wet, I was sure I would never dry off.

To distract myself, I practiced Morse code, which I needed to pass my amateur radio exam. My Morse code key made quite a racket. How in god's name would I remember that two dashes followed by a dot was a G, a dot followed by two dashes a W?

I was deep in concentration when I sensed rather than saw Dale standing at the door. She had come across the hall from her room. "How long are you going to be? I'm trying to study."

"Shut your door."

"I did. It's still loud."

"I can't help it."

Dale shifted her weight. "We have to come to some agreement. You practice all the time."

"What do you suggest?"

"A schedule. An hour a day. You pick the time."

"That's unfair."

"I have to study."

"Me too. I go to school too."

She leaned against the doorjamb. "Could've fooled me."

"That's completely unfair. I don't study as much as you, but who does?"

She pushed off the doorjamb. "I'm going to shut your door and mine and try to study. If I can't, I'll be back."

I sat at the makeshift table I had constructed out of a piece of plywood. I loved my sister but could only be in her presence for a few minutes

7007 Glenbrook Road, c. 1957. Tony's room, third floor, left window

before her nervous energy made me hum like a high-voltage line. She was 220 volt, I was 110. Action was her preferred state of being, quiet so I could think was mine.

Windows were my favorite feature of the room. The side window was inches above my bed, the front and back windows were gabled. I went to a window whenever my brain was stuck. Now I looked out across the backyard to the big tree at the fence. When I got my ham license, I'd need to string an antenna out the window to the tree. Which posed a problem. I'd have to climb the tree to secure the antenna, and I was terrified of heights.

—∭—

Memory rearranges events to tell a good story, much the way the dreaming mind attempts to make sense of nonsense. My memory of the chronology is hazy, but soon after Eisenhower was elected president, the Red-baiting senator, Joseph McCarthy, came to our house for dinner. McCarthy had begun his crusade against Communists in government but hadn't started frothing at the mouth yet. Eisenhower hoped to co-opt him, and enlisted my father's help. If anyone could win McCarthy over, it was Dad, who had wit and charm to spare.

McCarthy was a big man with a square face. I shook his beefy hand. At thirteen I knew little about politics but my instantaneous, indelible reaction was: This man is a thug, what is he doing in our house? Over the years, a lot of famous people came to our house—the admirable, the mediocre, and the creepy—but McCarthy was the only one who struck me as thug-like.

After dinner, he said he'd teach me boxing. I don't remember what precipitated the unwelcome offer. We went into the living room and he told me to raise my hands. He showed me how to punch and counter-punch. I remember him crouching and grunting, this big, beefy man who later terrorized Washington. Perhaps if I had been a better student and bopped his nose once or twice, McCarthy would have called off his Red-baiting crusade. I failed the nation, I'm sorry to say.

I wish my brothers and sister and I had shared our impressions of the famous people we met, held secret debriefings on the third floor, but we usually went our separate ways after guests departed. After routine family dinners, also. We ate together most evenings which meant late dinners since Dad didn't get home from work until seven or eight. Mother didn't do things halfway, including meals. She had a law degree from Cornell, but devoted her life to her husband and four children, as was the norm for many women of her era. Most evenings she prepared a full American meal, usually a roast of some sort, potatoes, vegetables, fresh fruit salad, sweet rolls, and dessert.

Dusk filtered through the trees into the dining room. The furniture was heavy and an oil painting of Mother's grandfather hung on the wall. My parents sat at the ends of the table, me adjacent to Dad, Doug next to me, Jeff and Dale across the table. If I looked straight ahead, I could see the street through the trees at the bottom of the front yard.

"I'm going to try out for the cheerleading squad," Dale said. She was a sophomore in high school.

"That's wonderful," Mother said. She had a patrician air about her, even at a family dinner. She was Dad's cheerleader, always keeping his interests foremost in her mind. As long as his interests were protected, she was the children's biggest supporter.

"Terrific, Dale," Dad said. He had light blond hair and a widow's peak. His smile was incandescent, his wit self-deprecating, his competitiveness unlimited. "If you make the squad, you can cheer Tony on when he makes the football team."

"I don't know if I'll try out," I said.

Dad's voice could cut like a scalpel when someone challenged him. I wanted his approval more than anything, and his tone reached my marrow. I had no defenses against it. As if I were born without skin. "Sports are the best preparation for life, I've told you that before. In the world of business or law, you need to know how good it feels to win and how bad it feels to lose. If you don't know how to win, you won't get ahead."

"I don't want to go into business or law." What I wanted to say but couldn't put into words even if I had found the courage to do so, was, I don't want to get ahead, I want to get out.

Dad's scorn skyrocketed. "Whatever you go into. Sports are a metaphor, a mirror of life. Pay attention."

Jeff was four years younger than I was and kept his thoughts to himself most of the time, but when he spoke, he spoke his mind. He was more athletic than I was. "I want to be on the football team," Jeff said.

"Good for you," Dad said. "Listen to your brother, Tony. He's got the right attitude."

"I didn't say for sure I wouldn't," I backtracked. "Sidwell's a small school and everybody tries out, so I may. You don't have to love football to make the team at Sidwell."

Dad exploded. He didn't yell when he blew, he grew exasperated, his

Adele Rogers

voice veering between hurt and scorn. How can you do this to me and how can you be so dumb? "You have to force yourself! You have to at least pretend to care. Once you get good at it, you'll love it."

Mother stepped in. "How was work today, dear?"

Dad sat back. The color in his face returned to normal. If he couldn't corral his wayward son, he could at least pontificate about his field of expertise. "The administration's starting to jell, but the press expects too much of Ike. Being a war hero works against him. He's a cautious man by nature. He wins by having a plan. I fear the press will turn on him when he doesn't storm the beaches in his first year." When Dad's nerves were on edge, he fiddled with whatever was at hand, a pen, a pencil. Now he fiddled with his fork, rolling it between his fingers as if he were performing card tricks. He swivelled his head from Mother to me. He locked his gaze on me. "Remember this, everyone will be gunning for you when you're on your own. No one will look out for you. You have to be ready. You have to be tough."

CHAPTER TWO

Girls

MY BEST FRIEND FLETCHER lived across the D.C. line in Georgetown. To get there meant a long walk, a bus ride to the D.C. border, and a long trolley ride. Fletcher lived in a townhouse.

"Are you going to try out for football next year?"

Fletcher didn't hesitate. "Of course, I can't wait. Are you?"

"I don't know. Maybe."

"Girls will like you better."

"Is that why you're going to do it?"

"Nah, I love football. I love to hit."

Fletcher was normally the gentlest of souls, but competition turned him into a beast. He was a scrappy runner, not tall, with short legs that moved faster than short legs have a right to move. Girls. That was a consideration to be kept in mind.

"Do you ever feel strange?" I asked. We were in Fletcher's third-floor bedroom. Even indoors, the city-feel of Fletcher's house was light years removed from our suburban Colonial with its big yard.

"In what way?"

"Not yourself. I feel like my own ghost sometimes."

"Puberty."

"It's that simple?"

"Dad's a Freudian. He believes sex explains everything."

Fletcher's dad was a psychiatrist. He saw his patients in an office on the first floor. I never saw the patients enter or leave, but knowing they were downstairs baring their souls made the house feel solemn and a touch scary.

"I want to learn guitar," I said.

"An even better way to get girls."

"Stop it. I'm serious. I want to sound like Les Paul."

Fletcher sang. "Somewhere there's music, how high the moon."

"I'm going to ask my mother if I can take lessons."

"Think she'll say yes?"

"She loves music. She's always listening to classical."

I was right. Mother answered my request with, "Of course, dear."

"Will Dad mind?"

"He won't care as long as you keep up your studies."

"I hate school."

"Don't let your dad hear that. He got out of Norfolk by doing well in school. He had no advantages in life, yet look what he's achieved. Don't argue with him that good grades aren't important."

"We live in a different time. I have different parents than he did."

"That's no excuse not to do your best."

Dad's mother died when he was thirteen. He never got along with his stepmother and was sent to live with his grandparents in Canton, New York, a town twenty-four miles from Norfolk, his birthplace. I can only imagine the feeling of loss and abandonment. Of being on his own before he was ready. Of only being able to count on himself.

The role of luck in our lives. Would Dad have been as driven if his mother hadn't died?

I started guitar lessons soon after that. I learned fast. My teacher said I was a natural.

—⁓—

Morse code was devilishly hard to learn. I couldn't imagine deciphering the dots and dashes at high speed. My third floor aerie became a sweat shop. Dale complained when she was in her room, but she was out doing school activities so often—Student Council, cheerleading tryouts, volunteering at a non-profit for children with disabilities—that I could tap away to my heart's content most of the time. I couldn't wait until I had an antenna strung out the window and a transmitter assembled and ready. I wondered how far my signal would reach. I had my eye on a Heathkit 25-watt transmitter to start. It would be easy to build and wasn't expensive. Twenty-five watts wouldn't reach around the world, I was pretty sure, but Europe? South America? Amazing to think of reaching Europe or South America from my room!

The guitar came easier than Morse code. I had no idea at first where to put my fingers, but I had no trouble getting my fingers to go where I wanted them to go. It was discouraging that I didn't immediately sound like Les Paul, but I loved the feel of a guitar. I could imagine how the strings would sound when I mastered them.

What chance did school have compared to music and shortwave radio? It wasn't that I lacked curiosity; I was intensely curious about the world outside Bethesda, but I wasn't interested in Charles Dickens or Colonial America. I wanted to know how things were made. I wanted to know how people lived. I wanted to know how I fit in.

Dinner. My stomach clenched, as it would before dinnertime until my mid-forties.

Roast beef tonight. Dad looking aggravated. "The press is so far off the mark about Eisenhower. You'd think they'd at least check their facts. Until I took this job, I didn't realize how far the standard story line can deviate from the facts."

I absorbed this lesson without conscious thought. I was readying myself for when Dad focused on me.

Dad had finished venting against the press. "Are you studying hard enough, Tony?"

"Yes."

"Adele says you're practicing your guitar a lot. Remember, you won't get anywhere in the world by playing guitar. Good grades will get you on the ladder, then it's up to you how high you want to climb."

"Where does the ladder lead to?" I didn't know why I always felt compelled to say something like that, why I didn't just nod.

Dad bristled. "Don't talk back. I know the world better than you. You won't stand a chance if you act like you're too good for it."

I shrugged. "I don't feel that way at all."

"Better men than you have tried to figure out the world, while everyone else raced by them. I didn't have your advantages when I was young. The house where I was born didn't even have running water. We had a pump in the backyard. Only when we moved across the street did we get indoor plumbing. Don't take your advantages for granted."

There was no answer that wouldn't sound snide or abject, so I shut up. I could see, across the table, a pained expression on my sister's face. Despite her highly strung nature, Dale had an aversion to tension. I looked at Mother at the end of the table. She was watching Dad intently.

"Well?" Dad said.

"I understand what you're saying," I replied.

"Good. That's settled then."

Doug, six years younger than me, two years younger than Jeff, sailed through family squabbles as if his boat was always on calm seas. "Someone please pass the salt," he said from his place next to me.

In my sanctuary after dinner, I tried to make sense of what had just happened. At the age of thirteen, I didn't have enough self-knowledge to compare and contrast myself with my father. Dad's central message—that getting ahead meant everything in life and that to get ahead you had to beat others at every turn—rang hollow to me. It may have been true during the Depression, but not in the prosperous fifties. There was enough to go around, the spoils did not go only to the "winners." And what constituted winning outside of sports or balance sheets, anyway?

I wasn't sure what I wanted to do with my life. The vague yearnings I felt didn't come with a label. The closest I could come to matching a word to them was the word "build." I liked putting things together—an Erector Set had been my favorite toy as a youngster—but "build" didn't quite match what I yearned for, and the word "create" hadn't yet entered my vocabulary.

Tony, age 13, 1954

I had just opened my history textbook when Dad knocked on my door. He didn't wait for me to say "come in" before he entered. I thanked my lucky stars I wasn't practicing Morse code. Dad kept his hand on the doorknob.

"You didn't take what I said at dinner seriously."

"I did. I understand what you're saying."

"But you think I'm wrong. Well, you'd save yourself a lot of trouble if you listened to me. But I guess it's human nature to have to learn the hard way."

"Dad, I'm studying."

"Your grades don't show it."

"I'll do better."

"You used to bring home great report cards."

"I'll do better."

Dad let go of the doorknob and stood in the doorway for a moment looking at me. "Goodnight."

I heard him going down the stairs. I waited until the footsteps stopped, then went to the door and closed it. I wished the door had a lock. The only room where I felt completely safe was the bathroom, which did have a lock.

I wanted to call Fletcher, but the only phones in the house were in the kitchen and my parents' bedroom. I didn't dare go down to the kitchen and risk Dad seeing me on the phone instead of studying. When I got my ham license, I'd be able to talk to people from my room.

Dad might be right about the importance of getting ahead, I admitted to myself. I couldn't see far enough into the future to know. But I thought not, and to preserve who I was until I knew for sure, I needed to come up with better defenses. Some way to protect myself from Dad without turning my back on him. Of course, one way would be to do what Dad asked. Study harder, play sports as if they mattered. Compete. Win. End of criticism.

Girls. Better than studying, better than sports. Where had they been hiding? Why hadn't I noticed them until now? I was tall, skinny, all elbows, knees, and ribs. I seemed without form or substance. If girls came close enough, they'd find they could stick their hands right through me.

Ham radio wouldn't attract girls, but maybe my guitar would. Or football! Football might win girls and Dad's praise.

CHAPTER THREE

Ham Radio

WHILE TEENAGE-ME struggled to find my identity, my father was advancing the cause of civil rights. He and Attorney General Herb Brownell recommended for the Federal bench legendary Southern judges like Frank Johnson and John Minor Wisdom (the best name ever for a judge, other perhaps than Learned Hand). These judges went on to overturn segregation laws that had stood since Reconstruction. Meanwhile, I made the junior varsity football team. As my mother used to say, "Huzzah!"

I should have tried out for receiver because I could catch, but I wanted to be the center of attention (girls), so I tried out for quarterback. Given that I weighed less than anyone who has ever played football, I had no body cushioning against the pain of being hit by someone twice my weight. Nor was I particularly good. But I won the position.

And I passed my ham radio exam. My license arrived in the mail on the day our team won for the first time that season. I opened the envelope as hurriedly as I could. My call letters were WN3BFW.

I told my mother about my license as soon as I opened the envelope. She seemed delighted. I didn't have a chance to tell Dad until dinner.

Dale had started the nightly dinner debate by saying she wished Eisenhower would speak out more passionately about civil rights. Mother saw trouble brewing and tried to divert the conversation. "Why don't you pass the rolls around the table, Dale."

I seized the moment to mention, "I got my ham license today. My call letters are WN3BFW." I don't know if a person can literally swell with pride, but my hunkered down inner self sure did.

"That's fine, Tony," Dad said. He turned his attention to Dale. "What more do you want Ike to do? He desegregated D.C., he's appointing good judges, we're drafting a civil rights bill that will be the first since Reconstruction. Ike doesn't shout. He just gets things done."

Dale cared passionately about civil rights and wasn't afraid to speak up. On the other hand, Dad cared as much about civil rights as she. I thought she sometimes picked fights in spite of her aversion to tension because it was the only sure way to get through to him. Offer our father a debate, and it was game on.

"The president sets the national tone. When Eisenhower speaks about civil rights, he sounds lukewarm. That's all I'm saying."

Dad bristled. "He's got a lot of constituencies, and he's cautious by nature. He didn't shout before D-Day, he prepared for it. What should he have done? Yell across the English Channel, 'ready or not, here we come'?"

Dale backtracked just enough to give Dad an opening. "I wasn't talking about D-Day."

"It's easy to sit back and criticize the men who are accomplishing things. Everyone thinks they can do better. I wonder if you'd have the courage to do what Ike's doing."

"We'll never know. I'm female."

"A woman could be president someday."

"Not in my lifetime."

"You'll never get ahead if you're a pessimist, Dale."

Dale burst into tears and bolted from the table. This happened often enough that no one was shocked. A brief, painful silence followed. I wondered, as always, if Mother would go and comfort Dale, but she stayed at the table.

I admired Dale. "I don't think she's a pessimist. If anything, I think she's too optimistic."

Tony with his ham radio set, Bill Rogers looking on. This photo was staged by the Weekly News Review, *1957.*

"Is that supposed to be clever?"

"It's supposed to say she's entitled to her opinion."

"As are you. But at least Dale's got a solid record. Student Council, honor roll, cheerleader."

"I forgot to mention. My football team won today."

Dad brightened. "You did? By how much?"

"Seven points. We won in the last quarter. I called a slant left. Caught the defense flatfooted."

"No kidding? Way to go." He looked at the other end of the table. "Isn't that great, Adele?"

"It is. It's wonderful."

"What's your team's record so far?" he asked me.

"1 and 5."

"Oh." His face readjusted from happy to how could you do so badly. "That's not good."

"Can't you be happy we won for the first time this season? Can't you be happy I got my radio license?"

"A losing season, and a ham radio license? Who's going to care?"

"Besides me, you mean?"

"The people you have to impress are the people who hold the keys to power. Impressing yourself is easy and irrelevant."

"How can I make you see?"

"See what?"

I wanted to join Dale in tears, but I was a guy. "Oh, never mind. Can I clear the table now?" That question was addressed to Mother.

"If Bill is through," she replied. "Are you, dear?"

"Not quite. But he can begin to clear."

At one point during the clean up, I was alone in the kitchen with Doug and Jeff. I kept my voice down, but I was angry. "Why didn't you two say something?"

Jeff shrugged. "What did you want me to say?"

Hard to argue with eight-year-old Doug's answer. "I was afraid."

—⁓—

I retreated to my room and shut the door. Above the fray, I fired up my newly built transmitter. Assembling it had been painstaking but fun. I grew fond of the smell of burning solder. The wisp of smoke that puffed up when I touched soldering iron to solder. I had mastered my fear of heights long enough to climb the tree and attach the antenna near the top. A long wire now extended out my window across the backyard to the tree. The antenna sagged in the middle. Now was the time to see if the setup worked.

CQ, CQ, DE WN3BFW—I tapped out the letters and number at slow speed, my proficiency still poor, even after hours of practice. CQ, CQ, CQ—anybody listening? Anyone want to make contact?

Then the answer came. Unmistakable. A distant signal tapping my call letters. It worked! I was too excited to remember where my first contact was calling from, but it was from somewhere in the Middle Atlantic states, not all that far. No matter. China could wait, I was content just to span distance with something I had built.

CHAPTER FOUR

Ping-Pong

OUR LIVING ROOM was comfortable, Woodward & Lothrop furniture, not formal as it later became. Off the living room was a much smaller room with a tile floor, where a ping-pong table had been set up.

Dad found me sitting on the floor in front of the living room record player listening to jazz. "I challenge you to a game of ping-pong." He said it in the formal tone a racetrack announcer uses to call horses to the starting gate.

I actually liked ping-pong but was engrossed in the music. "Not now, Dad." Inside, I was preparing to capitulate. I knew the drill. I'd have to play.

"Come on. I'll let you win."

"When have you ever done that?"

"Think you can't beat me?"

"Oh, okay." I uncrossed my legs and stood up. "Then can I go back to music?"

"If you're in one piece." Dad gave a good-natured chortle.

The thing that rattled me was that Dad didn't seem to take pleasure from a game, only the winning. Any competition seemed a fight to the death. I wondered what would happen if by some miracle I won: would Dad disappear in a puff of smoke?

Not to worry. I wasn't bad for my age, but I was no match for a seasoned gladiator. Dad had a vicious cross-table shot that forced me to lunge and return the ball off-balance. I had learned long ago that my only hope of survival was to play defense, which I wasn't bad at. I couldn't return Dad's shots with the needed intensity or precision to win, but I could keep the ball in play, on occasion long enough to frustrate Dad into grunts and grimaces. I relished these moments.

I lost the first game, and hoped Dad would be satisfied, but I knew better. "Come on, you're going to quit after one game? Best two out of three."

Not worth the effort to resist. "Okay."

"You serve."

"You won."

"It's okay. Serve."

Wonder of wonders, I won the second game. How did that happen? I asked myself. I was almost scared. The third game would be a killer.

"Nice game." Dad said. "Of course, I gave you the serve." He grinned widely. "Your serve."

I lost the third game by a wide margin. I was relieved. Dad played each point as if his life depended on it, and I didn't want to find out if it did.

Dad had worked up a slight sweat. "Another?"

I laid my paddle on the table. "No, Dad, I've had enough."

"You'll beat me sometime."

"Sure, Dad."

I didn't dare return to the living room and listen to more jazz. After such an intense battle, squatting cross-legged in front of the record player seemed like a wimpy thing to do, confirmation of everything Dad thought of me. A lack of fire. Insufficient fight. A lack of readiness for the world. Instead, I went upstairs to my room and opened a math book. I wanted to practice my guitar, but couldn't take a chance that Dad might climb the stairs to drum some lesson from the ping-pong game into my head. "Do you see what you're in for?" Dad might say. "You have to try much harder or you'll never get ahead." If I had a school book open, I stood a better chance of defusing him.

After twenty minutes without Dad appearing at the door, I crossed the room to my bed and picked up my guitar. Sitting cross-legged on the bed, I strummed a few chords. Quietly, so as not to alert Dad, nor draw Dale's ire.

—⁓—

I often took the bus-trolley combination to school. Sometimes Mother would drop me (and Dale, if she were going at the same time) at the bus stop on Wisconsin Avenue or the trolley at the District line, but other times I walked to the bus stop. The trolley ride through Northwest D.C. was long, the route winding, and afforded me plenty of time to think. Plus, there was no risk of Dad jumping on board and asking if I were getting ahead.

Sidwell Friends was a small, personal, Quaker school used to teaching the sons and daughters of Washington officialdom. The classes were minuscule, which was a good thing because the entire high school was housed in a wood frame building that had once been someone's home. The grounds sloped down from the high school, and on the downslope stood the middle school, a newer more-typical school building of brick. A gymnasium, bane of my existence, separated the two.

Fletcher and I were in many of the same classes, and whispered incessantly at the beginning of each year. By mid-year, we had been separated in all our classes. It didn't improve my concentration. The only class I truly liked was tenth grade English, taught by a tough taskmaster who drilled grammar into us after warning we'd hate him for it but thank him later. I liked grammar. There was a logic to it. Once you caught on to the logic, the rules of grammar made sense, and lent spine to what otherwise would be formless thought.

The second thing I liked about the class was that the teacher took breaks every so often to discuss questions that never got discussed in other classes. What was the meaning of life? Are humans social beings? Do books add anything to life? The teacher would give the discussion wide latitude but eventually steer it back to the book that had been assigned, a book which now took on new meaning as a result of being seen in a wider context.

After school, football. I met Fletcher outside the school every day to walk to practice, Fletcher gung-ho, Tony oh-no. "Why do you like this?" I groaned. The sky was overcast, rain likely. The field of battle muddy. I knew that by the end of practice, I would be covered in mud that no amount of showering would remove. "Why?"

Fletcher shrugged. "I like aimless violence."

"Get serious."

"Running and hitting. Evading tackles. I don't know."

Both of us tried out for varsity once we reached tenth grade. Fletcher made first string, I made third string.

Football camp was the worst. A week in the hot sun of Maryland's Eastern Shore before school started each year. Twice daily practices. Sweating (the conventional wisdom at the time: you shouldn't drink water while exercising because you'll get cramps). Dehydration. Sleeping in oversized tents.

What did Dad see in sports? I asked myself at night when I couldn't sleep. Maybe Dad valued sports because he didn't play them in high school or college. Too skinny. Well, I'm skinny, too, Dad, I wanted to say, though I never would. I wanted out from under the weight of his expectations, but didn't want to hurt his feelings. As much as I resented Dad, I sensed that he was a good man. I wanted his approval more than I wanted to bash him in the face.

In those rugged days, football players played both offense and defense. No namby-pamby platooning. Being 6 feet 1 inch tall and weighing 135 pounds (which remained true until my senior year), I was even less suited for defense than offense. To stop a 190-pound running back coming at you full speed it helps to weigh more than 135. Also, the collision hurts like hell, even if by some miracle, you do bring your man down. So when playing defense, I first and foremost defended myself. I hung back, got off a step too late, barely missed tackles. Darn! Almost had him.

One of our coaches was a brute named Butch. On the overcast day in question, doing my best to avoid contact while playing linebacker, I felt Butch sneak up behind me. When the ball was snapped and I didn't instantly lunge forward, Butch grabbed me by the hips and flung me towards the ballcarrier, turning me into an unguided missile. I brought down the runner but felt no triumph. Thoughts of murder entered my mind as I lay in the mud.

—◊◊◊—

Dad helped Richard Nixon when Nixon was serving on the House Un-American Activities Committee and Dad was a counsel for the Senate War Investigating Committee. When the House Un-American Activities Committee was deciding whether or not to prosecute Alger Hiss, Dad reviewed the evidence at Nixon's request and advised him to proceed, and when Nixon ran for vice president in 1952, Dad traveled with him as an adviser. The high or low point of the campaign was the infamous "Checkers speech," with its references to Pat Nixon's cloth coat and the gift of a dog named Checkers that the family would not give up no matter what. The speech preserved Nixon's place on the Eisenhower ticket.

Even at the age of twelve, I thought the speech was maudlin. Nixon had no shame, it seemed to me. I could not believe that my father had anything to do with it.

Nixon was a familiar presence in our house in my teens. He would come over for a drink after golfing with Dad at Burning Tree. Every so often it would occur to me that the man having a drink in our living room was the vice president of the United States, and mentally I would go "whoops, be on good behavior," but mostly he was just a friend of my father. He always wore a coat and tie. Nixon seemed as formal and awkward in private as he did in public. He made shy, uncomfortable me feel self-confident by contrast. When I tried to imagine what it must feel like to be him, I couldn't; there was nothing to latch on to. What torture it must have been for him to be constantly in the public eye. Why would a man uncomfortable in his own skin so relentlessly seek higher office? My adult guess is that the masochistic streak he displayed as president (taping his incriminating statements about Watergate, for example) was the dark side of his compulsion to seek high office. Reaching the pinnacle freed him to do himself in. A need for affirmation, a need for punishment, played out in the public eye. Nixon's life, as was said after his downfall, held elements of Greek tragedy, but in the fifties, he was just Dad's friend stopping by the house for a drink after a game of golf.

Dad was right, I should have studied harder. My lack of study skills hurt me badly when I later entered college. But I didn't see the point in high school. Laziness entered into it no doubt, although I wasn't lazy about my guitar or shortwave radio. I quickly became proficient in Morse code and passed the exam for a general license, which allowed me to drop the N from my call letters, and to use voice on the air. To use voice I needed a more powerful transmitter, so I built a 100-watt Heathkit which took up three times as much table space. My radio table was filling with equipment, and QSL cards covered the wall above the table, confirmations of contacts with other hams. My reach now extended around the world, and I took delight in entering contests to see how many states or countries I could contact in a given period of time.

I was equally diligent about my guitar and after two years of lessons formed a small band with some classmates. We were earnest but awful. But playing in a group speeded up my progress exponentially, and after two years of study and practice, I no longer needed to think about frets and fingers. My fingers knew what to do. All I needed to think about was the music. It was exhilarating.

My music career really took off in my sophomore year of high school. George, a friend from Sidwell, had recently joined a rock and roll band called The Rhythm Rockers, and he asked me to try out. I did, and joined the band. R&B was thriving but rock and roll was in its infancy, arguably started by Bill Haley and the Comets, "Rock Around The Clock." Our band modeled itself on Fats Domino. Bernie on saxophone led the band, with me on rhythm and solo guitar, George on piano, plus Shelly on bass and a drummer who looked like Ringo Starr. We clicked as a band immediately, our signature rhythm a shuffle beat (think "Blueberry Hill"). The band had been playing high school and country club dances for months before I joined, and soon we were playing

Tony playing guitar

every weekend. It was a heady feeling to be on a stage overlooking a sea of heads bobbing to our rhythm. Like being on the cover of *Parade* magazine, but this time due to my own efforts. I loved everything about playing in the band—the music, the tight-knit camaraderie among band members (we only had to glance at one another to know what the other was about to do), and the kick of seeing hundreds of people moving in time to our music. On occasion, everything came together, we were in sync and the crowd was in sync with us. When that happened, it was magic.

Watching people dance night after night convinced me of one thing: most people can't dance. Since I'm sure that includes me, I have been reluctant to dance ever since. We earned $125 a night, or $25 per person. In the fifties, that wasn't bad money, and I upgraded my equipment, buying a Gretsch sunburst guitar and better amplifier (although it was laughably puny compared to today's amplifiers). With the money I earned, I also amassed a sizeable collection of jazz recordings.

If I hadn't been a slacker about studying, I could've done all this and avoided Dad's scorn. He took no notice of my ham radio accomplishments or the rock and roll band; they flew under his radar. If I had better grades, I could've done both and remained in his good graces (well, there was still the sports thing), but I only studied enough to get by. My grades were mediocre, my teachers dismayed.

Given that I was going to disappoint Dad, I had to figure out how to protect myself. One way was to take on his coloring; like what he liked, agree with what he said. To some extent I did. There is a sort of Stockholm syndrome in a family. You can't pay a ransom and escape, so you take on the coloration of your captors. But I didn't want to lose the sense of who I was. I didn't want to be bent into someone I didn't want to be. I thought and thought and decided the only way to protect myself until I was old enough to leave home was to dig down as deeply as I could inside myself and hide. I couldn't escape but I could protect who I was by hiding my core under layers of self. I became two people: one available for others to know, one known only to myself. In the dark of my hiding place, I told myself to hunker down and wait until it was safe to come out. There is a price to pay for self-burial, however. When it comes time for exhumation, the soil may have hardened and be resistant to pickaxes and shovels.

For the record, being third-string quarterback on the Sidwell Friends football team does not attract girls. Nor does playing in a fifties-style rock and roll band (groupies had not been invented). I had a girl friend in ninth grade, a classmate of mine, but the more I withdrew, the less of me was available to her. Fletcher and I saw less of each other. My fault, my regret. Withdrawal becomes a habit hard to break.

—ɷ—

In September 1955, President Eisenhower suffered a heart attack after playing golf in Denver. Herb Brownell was out of the country, making my father the acting attorney general. Vice President Nixon sought my father's legal and political advice on what to do in the event Eisenhower couldn't carry out his duties. When the press outside the Nixon house became a crush, Nixon and my father decided to come to our house in Bethesda, where they would have more privacy, the question being how to get there without drawing the attention of the press. The solution they hit on was to have my mother drive over and wait on a side street while Nixon and my father snuck out the backdoor and across a neighbor's lawn.

I was on the third floor participating in an all-night shortwave contest when they arrived. When I went downstairs later to get a snack, Dad was on the phone in his bedroom and Nixon was on the kitchen phone receiving updates from Denver on Eisenhower's condition. I was immediately struck by how serious the atmosphere in our house was, as if the air had become heavier. I could almost feel it weighing on Nixon's shoulders. Eisenhower's prognosis was guarded, and Nixon was consulting with people inside and outside government on what duties he should assume while Eisenhower was in the hospital, and what to do in the event he died. He and Dad were on the phone far into the night, Nixon moving to the phone in my parents' bedroom, while my father took over the uncomfortable wall phone in the kitchen. I made several trips downstairs that night. I remember how awkward my usually graceful father looked leaning against the kitchen wall, leg bent, phone to his ear, jotting notes on a yellow legal pad that he had placed on top of the clothes dryer. I hadn't fully appreciated until then what Dad's job entailed.

Sometime during the early morning hours, Nixon and my father tried to get some sleep. Nixon was put in the bedroom directly below mine. I was wearing headphones and using a near-silent Morse code key, but in his book *Six Crises*, Nixon claims my dots and dashes kept him awake.

When I read that years later, I wondered why he didn't come up to the third floor and tell me to knock it off. He was the vice president, after all. What was I going to say? No?

Eisenhower eventually recovered and resumed his duties. I don't remember how I fared in the shortwave contest.

CHAPTER FIVE

Dale

DAD WAS THE DOMINANT figure in the family, but Mother was its heart and soul. She carried herself with quiet dignity. One wanted to stand straighter in her presence. It was impossible to imagine her shaving the truth, let alone lying, and equally impossible to imagine her ever being impolite. She treated everyone with respect. Her warmth was cloaked in good manners. Some people one wants to hug, Mother was the kind of person one wants to sit beside in order to bask in reflected warmth.

She was, in her way, as competitive as Dad. A field hockey player and runner in college, one of the first women admitted to Cornell Law School, she excelled at everything she did. She met Dad in law school and married him soon after graduation. As was the norm for a woman born in 1911, Mother never directly used her degree, devoting herself instead to her children and Dad's career. As long as her children were not in conflict with her husband, she was our biggest fan; my rock and roll band, my ham radio—she did not encourage me, but I knew she understood.

On a spring evening in Dale's final year at Sidwell, she and I were helping Mother in the kitchen, while Jeff and Doug set the table. Dale shared Mother's height, but her hair was curlier and brown to Mother's black. Dale almost buzzed with energy. "Mother, do you want this to go on the table?"

31

"Not yet, dear."

Dale picked up another serving dish. "This?"

"Not yet."

To kill time and to brag, I said, "I talked to Brazil today. My fiftieth country."

"Great," Mother replied.

"I'm going to run out of wall space if I get many more QSL cards."

"You must be very proud, dear."

I beamed.

Dale often speed-talked, as if she could not get her words out fast enough. "I went to see the headmaster today."

A brief flurry of worry crossed Mother's face. Dale saw it too. "I told you I was going to, Mother."

"And I'm proud of you. Does Bill know?"

"Not yet. I'll tell him at dinner."

"You mind telling me what's going on?" I asked.

"That serving dish is ready to go, Tony." Mother pointed at the mashed potatoes. "And Dale, you can take the carrots."

Jeff and Doug had set the table, salt and pepper shakers at each end, bread and butter plates at each place, cloth napkins in napkin holders. Dad had arrived home a few minutes before and had changed from his suit to a sports coat. He looked tired. Mother was the last to sit down.

"How was today, dear?"

"I went to the Hill to unstick the civil rights bill. We're running into more resistance, and not just from the usual suspects." He took his napkin out of its ring and placed it on his lap. He had fixed himself a Scotch before he went upstairs to change, and now took a sip. "To listen to the bill's opponents, you'd think we were proposing to abolish the white race."

Mother encouraged him. "One hundred years without a civil rights bill is long enough."

"Exactly."

Dale asked, "Is Eisenhower fully behind it?"

Dad frowned. "Of course, do you think Herb and I would do this without his support?"

Dale, age 16, 1953

"It's just that I read in the papers … ."

Dad clenched his fist but didn't bang the table. He didn't have to. "Don't … do not … believe everything you read. The Washington press corps swoons for its own rhetoric. Eisenhower may be pragmatic, but he knows what's right. He ended segregation in D.C., he's appointing open-minded judges, he's pushing the first civil rights bill since Reconstruction. What more does the press corps want?"

"I went to see the headmaster today."

"Did you hear me, Dale? Don't believe everything you read about Eisenhower. He isn't getting a fair shake."

"I understand, Dad. Can I tell you what I said to the headmaster?"

"Remind me, why did you go see him?"

"That's what I'm trying to tell you."

"Okay. Go ahead."

"I told him that Sidwell Friends should admit Negroes. I said that for a Quaker school not to enroll Negroes is shameful."

"Did he get angry?"

"I don't think he's used to students talking to him like that."

"I'll say. Did you think of what this might do to your future?"

"I thought you'd be proud."

"You know I'm for civil rights, but you're applying to college."

"Dad, I'll get into college. I've got great grades. I'm applying to Cornell. They'll let me in."

"But will you come highly recommended?"

"*Dad?*"

"I know you've done well, but I want you to enter college with every possible advantage. I'm only thinking of you."

Tears came to Dale's eyes. "I thought you'd be proud."

Mother stepped in, gently. "Think of how brave this was for Dale to do."

"It was brave. But Dale has to look out for herself."

Dale lost it. She ran from the table and up the stairs, her sobs fading the higher she got, until a door slammed on the third floor and there was silence.

"I wouldn't have the guts to do what she did," I mumbled.

Dad ignored me. He stared at Mother. "I'm concerned about her future, is that so wrong?"

"No, dear, I am too."

"It's a tough world out there, and she's a woman. It's going to be harder for her."

"I know."

"She has to weigh the good she can do by angering the headmaster versus the harm she can do to herself."

"You're right, dear."

Dad sat back and paused. "Did you say something, Tony?"

I didn't have the guts to repeat what I had said, nor the good sense not to say what I did. "I notched my fiftieth country today. Brazil."

For a moment, Dad looked confused. "What does that have to do with what I'm saying?"

"Nothing. I just thought you'd want to know."

Upstairs after dinner, I knocked on Dale's door. "Can I come in?"

"Go away."

I opened the door an inch. "I brought you the rest of your dinner."

Dale sniffed. "Why is he so mean?"

"I'll bet he doesn't think he's mean."

"He's hard on you, too."

I opened the door enough to see Dale sitting cross-legged on her bed. "And when he is, I hate him."

"Don't say that."

"Here, take this." I handed Dale the plate.

"The headmaster didn't seem angry. Surprised but not angry. He thanked me before I left."

"Good for you."

"Do you think Dad will ever be proud of me?"

"I think he already is."

Dale looked at her food. "Why are you being so nice?"

"Because I don't have your guts."

"But you're being nice about Dad, too."

"You didn't hear the stupid thing I said after you left the room."

"What did you say?"

"None of your business. Goodnight." I shut the door and crossed the hall to my room, where I switched my radio gear on. While I waited for the tubes to heat up, I wondered what the atmospheric conditions were like tonight. Maybe I'd snag number fifty-one.

My guess is that we die as ignorant as the day we are born, we just accumulate habits of mind along the way. Looking back on my mid-teens, I am struck by how certain I was that Dad was unfair. Period. There was no wiggle room in my belief.

—⁂—

Tony's paternal grandparents, Myra Beswick Rogers and Harrison Rogers

I was aware of the basic facts about Dad's childhood. He was born in Norfolk, New York, in 1913. His father was a supervisor in one of the paper mills attracted to the far northern reaches of New York State by the water power of the St. Lawrence River. When the paper mill closed, Dad's father opened an insurance agency serving Norfolk, Canton, and the surrounding towns of St. Lawrence County. Jeff and I drove to Norfolk not long ago to revisit the town. The insurance agency is still there, run by the grandson of Dad's stepmother. The town itself seems so fragile as to be at risk in a high wind. My adult self is awed by the hard work and luck that must have gone into Dad's climb from such modest beginnings. My teenage self didn't care. Dad was unfair, and that was that.

He was also self-deprecating, which made it hard to stay angry at him. He once told a story about being on the road after he had taped *Meet The Press* and wanting to see the program when it was broadcast. This was in the fifties and the hotel where he and his aide were staying didn't have TV, so he located a nearby hotel that did. When Dad asked the aide if he wanted to walk the three blocks to see him on TV, the aide said, "Bill, I wouldn't walk three blocks to see you in person."

Herb Brownell resigned in 1957, and President Eisenhower appointed my father attorney general. In person Eisenhower resembled a kindly but intimidating grandfather. I remember standing next to him after Dad's swearing in and chatting about my high school football team, thinking, "This is very strange." I had just come from practice. I had showered before leaving for the White House but hoped that body odor wasn't the cause of Eisenhower's look of mild annoyance.

Dad's transition to his new job was smooth and didn't make much difference in the family's life. By then we were used to the Washington fishbowl. Dad was assigned a government limousine which meant rides to school in the morning, but my brothers and I were embarrassed for our classmates to see us in a limousine and always asked to be dropped off a few blocks away.

Nixon continued to stop by our house after golf, sometimes staying for dinner. I usually had nothing to say to him other than pleasantries, not knowing what to say and not wanting to make a fool of myself, but one time I thought, "I have to take advantage of this opportunity," and asked him a foreign policy question. He was sitting across the table from me, looking comparatively relaxed for a man in a sport coat and tie. I don't remember the question but I remember the vice president visibly stiffening, as if the question came from a hostile journalist at a press conference. He answered in long, formal sentences with awkward pauses and not much specific information. I was stunned. I was a know-nothing seventeen year old asking an innocuous question in the privacy of his friend's home. He had nothing to fear, but he treated my question as a time bomb. He was more insecure than I.

Yet he had responsibilities I could only imagine. I remember the time Doug and I rode with Nixon and Dad to a Baltimore Colts football game. Riding with the vice president was a much bigger deal than riding to school with my father. Nixon's limousine was surrounded fore and aft by Secret Service vehicles, and a Secret Service agent riding shotgun in the limo was in constant radio communication with the others. I remember

Nixon and Dad talking politics during the ride. Doug remembers they discussed Nelson Rockefeller. I listened with half an ear, more fascinated by the radio chatter than the politics. But at some point I became aware that they were discussing a foreign policy issue that Nixon had the power to do something about. The discussion wasn't theoretical or hypothetical, it was as real as real can be, and I felt a weight on my shoulders just listening to them. If you haven't felt that pressure, don't be too glib with your criticisms. Not that that stopped me.

When we reached the Baltimore city limits, a phalanx of Baltimore motorcycle cops surrounded our motorcade and sped us through the streets at alarming speed. I had the distinct impression that they enjoyed an excuse to roar through the city. There was a little-boys-with-machines aspect to their speed. At one point, an old woman stepped off the curb just as the entourage roared by and Nixon's limousine almost clipped her. He was visibly shaken and ordered the Secret Service to slow down. We reached the stadium without killing anybody, and were hustled to our seats by the Secret Service and Baltimore Police. I remember how rough they seemed, shoving people out of the way if necessary. My guess is protocol calls for constant forward movement in order to reduce the danger presented by a stationary target.

CHAPTER SIX

The Rhythm Rockers Go To Europe

THE CIVIL RIGHTS BILL that my father had worked on for years, the first civil rights bill since Reconstruction, finally became law in September of 1957 after overcoming a marathon filibuster by Senator Strom Thurmond, the longest in Senate history. In December, as one of his first acts as attorney general, Dad created the Civil Rights Division of the Justice Department. The civil rights bill opened the door to stronger bills, and the Civil Rights Division meant that the Justice Department now had staff devoted entirely to the enforcement of civil rights.

In theory, I was thinking about college. My sister had chosen Cornell, where she was excelling. I had to apply soon but had no burning desire to go. I had ruled out business, law, or medicine as professions, which (in my myopic world view) left only engineering. I liked ham radio, did I not? I loved to tinker, was fascinated by electronics. Ergo, electrical engineering. Like I say, no burning desire, but at least a direction.

Meanwhile, the Rhythm Rockers were thriving. We played at a Penn State fraternity party, where Bernie took it into his head to jump out the rear window of the room while wailing on his saxophone, run around the house, and appear triumphantly at the front door, still honking away. We bought matching red sports coats, which made us look like backup singers in a Motown group, and which we thought made us look cool.

Dwight D. Eisenhower with Bill Rogers, 1957

Our big break came in the spring of my senior year. We were offered a regular gig at a Maryland bar, east of D.C. Because we would be playing at the same place every week, and because it was not a high school or college dance, we would get exposure, followed quickly by fame and fortune. We were thrilled beyond words. Our dreams had come true, our ship had come in, only in America, etc, except if your father is attorney general and oversees the FBI. He told me, "Tony, I need to have that bar checked out. It would be damaging to me if your name gets in the papers for the wrong reasons."

The FBI conducted a background check of the bar (what other rock and roll band can say that? The Rolling Stones? The Ramones? I think not) and reported that the police frequently raided the bar for serving liquor to minors and to break up fights. Reluctantly, Dad told me I couldn't play there. "If you're playing in a bar that's raided by the police, it'll get in *The Washington Post*, and it would make it harder for me to do my job."

I was outraged. Incredulous. Hatred, fury. Move over, Achilles, your wrath was as nothing compared to mine. I couldn't argue with my father that it wouldn't get in the papers, I knew he was right. Nor could I argue it wouldn't damage him, but only temporarily, while my musical career would die. But he was adamant. And to give him his due, he sounded truly reluctant when he broke the news.

I hated to tell the rest of the band. I didn't know if they would hire another guitarist or sacrifice the gig, but either way, something that had nothing to do with them would affect them. I can't recall how I told them or what they immediately said. In the end they decided to give up the gig, and continue the band intact. Bless them.

As it turned out, the gods of rock and roll were looking after us. More powerful than the FBI, those gods. The Rhythm Rockers were hired to play on an ocean liner to Europe that summer. Not quite fame and fortune, but a free trip to Europe.

But before summer came, I had to decide about college. I had applied to several engineering schools, including MIT, and been accepted by all. Why I don't know, given my grades. I had good SATs and teacher recommendations along the lines of "lots of untapped potential, with proper motivation can do well," plus as my wife reminds me, it didn't hurt my chances that my father was attorney general of the United States.

Scared to death, feeling out of my league even before I started, I chose MIT. Engineering was not in the family orbit, so going to MIT seemed surreal, so surreal that I can't remember my parents' reaction. Was my father proud? Did he congratulate me for my 'win'? You'd think I'd remember. I'm sure my mother said, "Wonderful, dear," and I'll bet my father said nice things, but my radar only picked up criticism from him, not praise, and if he congratulated me, it didn't register.

In my senior year I sang the lead in our high school musical, Kurt Weill's American folk opera, *Down in the Valley.* In prior years I had sung in the chorus for *Carousel* and *Brigadoon* and had minor roles in a couple of dramas. I don't think it's unusual for shy people to act. Just as I had split myself into two people and hidden one of them internally as a kind of disguise, acting gives a shy person a character to hide behind.

My most vivid memory of the play was rehearsing a scene where I was singing a joyful soliloquy alone on stage (I had just kissed the girl I longed for). The drama coach instructed me to stretch out my arms and twirl around, singing at the top of my lungs. I complained to her, "Isn't that going to look corny?" To which she replied, "Tony, only a third of what you do onstage will make it across the footlights."

I got lots of pats on the back after the performances, but I sensed they were more for Brack Weaver, my character, than for me. Brack Weaver was a really sweet guy. I liked him, too. On his behalf, I accepted the congrats.

In the spring, Robert Frost visited our house to thank my father for his help in getting Ezra Pound released from St. Elizabeths psychiatric hospital, where Pound had been confined in lieu of going to jail for supporting fascism in Italy during World War II. My mother took me and my brothers out to the front patio to meet Frost. He and my father sat looking out across the front lawn, Frost with his white hair instantly recognizable even from the side. I was not a big reader of poetry at the

Poster depicting the Arosa Star, *1957*

time, but Frost's reputation made him more daunting to me than vice presidents or senators. Anyone could be a politician, only the rare few could write books. My brothers and I mumbled our hellos and soon were ushered back inside.

—ɯ—

The Rhythm Rockers showed up at dockside with our instruments the day we were to embark from New York on the *Arosa Star*. Only problem was our names were not on the passenger roster. We didn't know what to do. Turn around, take the train home? Admit defeat? Finally, we reached the family friend of one of the band members, the man who had arranged the whole thing, and he straightened it out with the shipping company. The ship was one of three or four small ships owned by a company that has since gone out of business for failure to pay taxes. We didn't know that at the time, of course, all we knew was that we were on board and ready to set up our instruments, don our red jackets, and rock.

Playing on a ship turns out not to be much different than playing at a high school except there's an ocean outside. The age range of our audience was greater than we were used to, but there were plenty of young people. The crossing was uneventful. It took ten days, which says something about the size and speed of the ship. We disembarked in Bremerhaven, Germany, and had two weeks to see Europe. I made it as far as the city of Bremen, forty miles to the south, where we planned to stay overnight.

After dinner I got violently ill and spent the night in the shared bathroom of the cheap hotel we were staying in. A doctor was summoned, and I was diagnosed with appendicitis.

I called my parents from the hospital. Since I was a minor, I needed their permission to operate. I woke them (it was 3 a.m. in Bethesda). They were concerned and supportive, but I was scared.

Few people spoke English at the hospital. The doctor who stopped to see me once a day spoke English, but none of the nurses did. I was in serious pain the first day or two but didn't know how to ask for a painkiller. Also I'm shy about asking for things for myself.

My friend George, the piano player—bless him—stayed in Bremen the whole eleven days I was in the hospital, missing his chance to see Europe. He visited my room twice a day and made me laugh, but any movement of my abdomen was agony, and George was a very funny man. Did he stop when I asked him to? He did not. Bless him anyway.

The band reunited in Bremerhaven for the return trip only to discover that the shipping company had no plans to get us home. The only ship leaving anytime soon had been chartered by the Jehovah's Witnesses to carry two thousand of their followers to The Divine Will International Assembly at the Polo Grounds and Yankee Stadium in New York. We screamed and hollered and told them of my operation, and they finally said we could hitch a ride with the Witnesses.

By that point we just wanted to get home and didn't care who we played for. Which was lucky because Jehovah's Witnesses considered rock and roll to be the devil's music and listening to it a sin. We played every night to a handful of off-duty crew members. But we played.

Then we hit a hurricane. The ship, being small, had no chance against the waves, and soon the deck was lined with people vomiting over the railings into the sea. There were times when the railings were so crowded, you had to use your elbows or wait your turn. Still, we played.

The ballroom windows stretched around the stern of the ship. From the bandstand, we could see ocean and sky out the stern, normally half and half of each, but during the hurricane, the ship bucked and reared so violently that at one moment we'd see only sky, the next only ocean. Bottles and glasses fell from the bar and crashed to the floor. The drummer vomited during a song. Still, we played. Through a hurricane that lasted several days.

We only missed one beat. It happened when the ship rolled so violently that the drummer's hi-hat cymbal fell over. I was sitting facing him, with my legs crossed to balance my guitar, and reached out with my foot to stop the hi-hat from hitting the floor. But we dropped a beat. One missed beat through hurricane and hellfire. Give it up for the Rhythm Rockers.

We later decided that the hurricane was a sign that the Witnesses were right about rock and roll.

When the seas calmed and the railings had been cleaned of vomit, we were standing on the open deck getting some air when George said a casual hello to a young Jehovah's Witness woman standing near us. A conversation of utmost innocence ensued, George not being of the lecherous type, when a Jehovah's Witness elder approached. He seemed benign, but when he got close, he hauled off and punched George in the jaw, then led the young woman away without a word. We stood stock still, too stunned to react.

Suffice it to say that none of us spoke to any of the young women on board after that. We did talk to some of the young men, who tried without success to convert us. Maybe if an elder hadn't punched one of us in the face, their proselytizing would've stood a better chance.

—⁂—

While the Rhythm Rockers were still in Europe, Edward R. Murrow featured my family on his popular TV show, *Person To Person*. Watching the black-and-white tape of the broadcast now is to see my parents walk as stiffly as if on stilts and talk as if they were lip-synching to a pre-recorded script. Television can hijack the personalities of even the most polished people.

Murrow asks my mother to introduce the children to him, which she does. Then Murrow says he understands the oldest son is in Europe, is that right? Mother holds up my high school graduation picture. "Yes, it is, Mr. Murrow. This is our son, Tony. He and his band, the Rhythm Rockers, are playing on a boat to Europe this summer."

The camera cuts to Murrow, leaning back in his chair in the television control room. He puffs on his cigarette. "Isn't that interesting," he says.

CHAPTER SEVEN

I Meet John Coltrane

I WAS NOT DEVOID of ambition. I knew I couldn't match Dad's drive and competitiveness, but I wanted to do something meaningful, and I wanted to beat my father. For a young man who deplored his father's ultra-competitiveness, wasn't that hypocritical? The difference between Dad's competitiveness and mine was that Dad wanted to beat everyone, I only wanted to beat Dad. And the competition wasn't the rah-rah, we're number one stuff: there was a paying homage by getting in the ring with the old man aspect to it, a great things are expected of first sons aspect, and a payback for all the crap aspect. Complicated, and yes, hypocritical.

I rested at home for the remainder of the summer, my appendectomy scar a reminder of the wages of sin. The more I thought about MIT, the more afraid I became. I was woefully ill-prepared, and in the inner cave where my true self hunkered down, I knew that. On the surface, I was super confident.

"Are you ready?" Dad said at the dinner table mid-summer.

"You bet."

"Good to hear."

The windows were open to let in what little breeze there was, but high humidity weighed the breeze down like an anchor, and it didn't make it across the dinner table to me. Dale was home for the summer and raving about Cornell. Joined this, won that, did well, want to help others. Oh, give me a break, Dale. The damn thing was she wasn't bragging. She never bragged. It was always about seeking Dad's approval, and as usual he listened to Dale with approval but a short attention span. Dale was a girl, and girls were not expected to do as well in the world as boys. If they did, great, Dad was all for it. But it didn't loom as large in his eyes as Jeff's or my accomplishments. Too bad I didn't have any, except getting into MIT. Jeff had plenty. In his first year of high school, he had been a star on the JV football team, won a prize at a junior science fair, and in general carried himself with the kind of quiet confidence and drive that both Dad and I could applaud. So far, young Doug seemed to have escaped the family pressures, the nine-year age gap between Dale and Doug apparently inhibiting trickle-down expectations.

My bedroom got hotter than hell in the D.C. summers. I opened all the windows and propped a box fan in the window by my bed, and the front and back dormers caught any stray breezes, but Dale and I roasted on the third floor. I kept up my radio contacts in spite of the heat generated by my equipment. MIT had a ham radio club, I learned from the catalog, but it wouldn't be the same as my own radio in my own room with its wall full of QSL cards and the wire antenna strung across the backyard to the tree I had heroically climbed.

Why do we have to change? I had wanted out for so long, but now the prospect lost appeal. Stay put. Keep your head down. Don't move and maybe no one will notice you. When you're at MIT, who knows how you'll do?

—∿∿—

MIT prides itself on numbering its buildings instead of naming them—Building 6, Building 10, Building E23, and so forth. Its industrial-strength campus anchors one long stretch of Cambridge along the Charles River. I and most other freshmen pledged fraternities upon arrival. My fraternity house was on the Boston side of the river. To go back and forth from fraternity to campus meant long cold walks over the Harvard Bridge, best known for being 364.4 smoots long (Oliver

The Harvard Bridge, 364.4 smoots long, c. 1959

Smoot was a pledge used by his fraternity as a human ruler to measure the length of the bridge).

Sidwell Friends had been the Boy Scouts; MIT was the Marine Corps. I felt hopelessly lost almost from the start. I lacked the study skills to keep up with the massive onslaught of homework, I lacked the higher math skills required for engineering, and I had a hard time maintaining my enthusiasm for the fraternity. I had just met these people, yet was supposed to pledge eternal brotherhood? In panic, I turned to women and music. My girlfriend was a beautiful Simmons student who did not pass judgment on me when I confessed to floundering at school. In high school, girls had been my comfort and solace, my two safe places being the company of women and my internal hiding place. The young women I was drawn to were for the most part quiet, non-judgmental, and brunette. Like my mother, but since I had never been confident Mother would support me if I were in conflict with Dad, I preferred arm's length relationships with girlfriends.

And I turned to music and radio. I joined the campus radio station and was given a weekly late night show which I dubbed, "Just Jazz." I had brought to MIT a sizeable portion of my jazz collection and put serious thought into what I played and in what order. Should Sonny Rollins come before or after John Coltrane? Or should I separate them with some Stan Kenton?

Mid-term grades were given to MIT freshmen so they could see where they stood. The grades didn't count in the end but were an indicator. My mid-term grades were three F's, a D, and a C.

How would I tell my parents?

The long walks across the bridge became even longer. Winter comes early in New England, and the wind was often biting, the cold black waves forbidding. It was sleeting one morning as I walked across, and I angled my head to keep the sleet out of my eyes. I felt as low as I had ever felt. Often in high school, I had felt alone in a permanent, unalterable sense, but here I realized I hadn't experienced the worst of it.

If I flunked out, how could I face Dad?

Dad and my high school grades had made me feel dumb, my MIT mid-terms confirmed it. Everything seemed black. The wind swirled. Suicide did not seem out of the question. Water seemed safer than air.

It would be easy.

It was not the last time I thought of jumping as I walked across the bridge.

Safe for the time being on the other side, I regrouped. I sought help from a counseling dean, I ditched the jazz show to devote all my time to my studies. But I had fallen too far behind to catch up. Math is cumulative.

The final thing I could try was moving out of the fraternity. The atmosphere had come to seem stifling, and the activities too time-consuming. I discussed it with the fraternity's officers, who discouraged me.

"Isolating yourself won't help," one of them said.

"If you can't make it with our support, you can't make it outside," another said.

"Think of your future, do you want to have 'quitter' on your resumé?"

I went back to my room, which I shared with another pledge. My roommate was out at the time, which was fortunate, because I felt like crying. "Quitter" had rung a bell. I remembered drying dishes in the Bethesda kitchen one evening early in junior high when it hit me all of a sudden that I didn't have Dad's hunger to win and could never compete with him and had quit trying. I quit. I was a quitter.

I was sitting on my bed when I remembered the guilt I had felt then. I was sure now, with failure at MIT on the horizon, that a sense of myself as a quitter had contributed to my certainty that something was fundamentally wrong with me, and that no one would like me if they got to know me. I got off the bed and left the room. Downstairs was quiet. A few fraternity brothers were studying in the living room. My brothers studied very hard during the week and got very drunk on Saturday nights.

I crept out the door. As soon as I was outside, I knew I had to quit the fraternity, no matter what that confirmed about me. If I were to go down, I had to do it on my own, in my own way.

I walked along darkened Bay State Road, freezing my butt off, until my resolve was firm. The next day I went to the housing office and applied for a dorm room.

I felt relief once the decision was made, and packed up my things. On my last morning at the fraternity, I awoke to find a note had been slipped under my door during the night. The note contained one word: "Quitter."

—⁂—

Deliverance came in the form of disease. Just before Christmas, I felt as if a boulder had taken up permanent residence in my stomach. For several days I couldn't eat, and when I looked in the mirror, I discovered that overnight my skin had turned bright yellow.

I spent the next few days in the MIT infirmary, diagnosed with hepatitis A, and shipped home to recover. I was one sick puppy.

Two benefits from getting sick: I never received final grades for the semester, so technically didn't flunk out of MIT, and I was so sick when I got home that I was oblivious to Dad.

For six weeks, I lay flat on my back in bed, lacking the energy to read, watch TV, or even think. To get out of bed and walk to the bathroom required many minutes of psyching up. Eleven days in a German hospital with only George for company, six weeks in bed at home oblivious to everything except the slow passage of time.

I was no good at studying but a Phi Beta Kappa at silence.

I was really sick. Attempts at perspective aside, I felt really horrible. Once I recovered enough to spend time out of bed, it took weeks before I recovered a semblance of my former energy. Eventually I did, but by then the first semester and part of the second were gone. I had blown my freshman year. I had no idea what I wanted to do in lieu of engineering, but one thing for certain, I was never going back to MIT even if they would take me.

I found a job at NBC's Washington studios as a page, giving tours of the building to visitors, delivering mail, manning the telephone switchboard at lunch (I once inadvertently severed a call from the president of NBC).

George, the piano player, was still in town, and he and I hung out together at night. One night we went to the Crosstown, a cocktail lounge on Mt. Pleasant Street off 14th. A quiet jazz trio, Three Kings And A Queen, was playing on a cramped, raised stage. A sultry singer added a smoky touch to the intimate room. It was a place where people who wanted background music for their conversation went to drink. No riots there.

George knew the piano player, a hefty middle-aged African American, and was asked to sit in. He played one song, then I sat in.

The guitarist was Charlie Byrd's brother. Charlie Byrd was a well-known jazz and classical guitarist who had his own nightclub in Georgetown. To sit in for Charlie Byrd's brother was an honor.

I must have done okay because when I finished, the piano player asked if I wanted a job every Friday and Saturday, 9 p.m. until 2 a.m. It turned out Charlie Byrd's brother was leaving the band, and the piano player, the bandleader, was looking for a replacement.

By now the FBI surely was used to checking out bars where I was to play. I wouldn't be surprised if they established a separate division to check on my venues. Dad had the Civil Rights Division to his name, I had the Dive Bar Unit. The Crosstown apparently passed muster because Dad gave me his okay. Postscript: after I began playing, I learned that the bar regularly served underage drinkers. That's why so many young people flocked there. No riots but plenty of scofflaws. Months after I started, *The Washington Post* learned the attorney general's son was playing at the Crosstown and sent a photographer to catch me in the act. It wouldn't have done my father harm because the bar didn't have a bad reputation, but I didn't want that kind of attention, so I asked the bouncer at the door to block anyone with a camera. The photographer showed up but couldn't push his way in, which led to wild celebration by the band and bartenders, who by then were in on the plot.

In order to play at the Crosstown, I had to join the musicians' union. D.C. had been desegregated for only six years and plenty of remnants of segregation remained, including two musicians' unions, a de facto white union and a de facto black union. My band mates, who were black, said they'd take me to their union hall to sign me up. Which is how I became a member of the black musicians' union.

Slowly, over the next few months, I regained my strength. I wasn't one hundred percent but I could stay on my feet for five hours on the bandstand. It wasn't a chore, it was sheer joy. The other members were so much better than I it wasn't funny, but I learned to fake the songs I didn't know and held my own on the blues in B flat and standards like "Early Autumn," which became the band's break song.

Playing alongside Butch Warren, the bassist, was the greatest joy. We were the same age, if not the same ability, and would go to his house to jam after the gig was over for the night. Other musicians would often join us. Butch went on to become a renowned bassist, playing with such jazz greats as Thelonius Monk, Dexter Gordon, and Herbie Hancock, but for the moment, he was just my friend. At the Crosstown, I was aware of how lucky I was to listen to him solo night after night. He had some riffs he played on the rare occasions he ran out of inspiration. The riffs, repeated rhythmic patterns, swung like hell, and always got a rise from the crowd. But he knew and I knew the riffs meant he had run out of ideas, and when he resorted to them, we laughed ourselves silly.

He took me to clubs where I might not have gone myself, given the de facto segregation which still existed. One afternoon, John Coltrane, already a legend, was playing a matinee at a small basement club, and Butch and I went to hear him. Coltrane was blistering, as usual. He played with an intensity and musicality that made it seem like nothing mattered except squeezing all possible notes out of a chord.

Butch knew a member of the band, and at break, they spoke. When Butch returned to the table, he told me he had been invited to sit in. He was almost hyperventilating. Butch was a calm guy, and I worried. "Are you okay?"

"Tony, I know what they're going to do." Jazz musicians are very competitive (my father may have been a jazz musician in a prior life), and Butch was sure they'd try to cut him. He tapped his palms together at warp speed to illustrate. "They'll play this fast. I *know* it."

He was right. The song they played when Butch sat in was so fast there were no intervals between beats. But Butch did just fine.

When the song ended, he was visibly relieved. He had no breath left when he sat, and could only nod when I said, "Way to go."

Coltrane sat down at a nearby table when the band took a break. "Come on, I'll introduce you," Butch said.

Introduce me to God, he might have said. I approached, with Butch as my cover. Coltrane was sitting sideways, his face sweaty.

Butch introduced us, and I shook Coltrane's hand.

"And now, Tony, you can say you met John Coltrane," Butch said.

Coltrane had a gentle handshake and an even gentler smile. He smiled up at me from his chair. "And now I can say I met Tony Rogers."

CHAPTER EIGHT

Sometimes You Have To Yell

THE STRANGEST PART of the six months I played at the Crosstown was how removed I felt from my family even though I was living at home. Working at NBC during the day, playing the club late into the night on weekends, I had entered a parallel universe. The fuzziness associated with recovering from a serious illness added to the sense of dislocation.

The year was 1959, pre-Martin Luther King, pre-the civil rights marches of the sixties, when racism was still a palpable daily presence, yet the band accepted me as a musician. I had no skin color. On our breaks, my bandmates would chat about daily difficulties, minor indignities, and the routine nature of coping with racism. Daily-type gossip, not rants. The talk was casual, who did what to them, what barriers they had run into that week. Racism was such a familiar part of their lives it was just another thing they coped with. I was struck by how openly and without bitterness they talked about it, and never, not once, did they preach to me.

The raised bandstand we played on was bathed in an overhead light that turned both black and white skin a weird dark purple. A former Sidwell student I slightly knew entered the bar one night, saw me on the bandstand and remarked to his girlfriend, "That black guy on guitar looks like Tony Rogers."

During my six months at the Crosstown, I gave serious thought to music as a career. I enjoyed it more than anything else I did, and now that engineering was out of the question, I had no other aspirations. Music is a hard life, the hours nocturnal, and many of the musicians I met during those six months used heroin. Yet I loved playing. Music justified everything, and one didn't have to be a jazz giant to earn a living. My guitar teacher earned a living by playing locally and teaching. That was doable.

I received occasional encouragement from people who came to the club. As I stepped down from the bandstand on an otherwise unremarkable night, a young man complimented my guitar playing. "You're as good as Charlie Byrd!" he enthused. Not true, not even close. But nice to hear. Another night I was approached by a middle-aged man who asked me to join him at his table on break. He had recently become the owner of a nightclub down the street and made me an offer. "I'm hiring a house band. Would you like to lead it?"

No need to mull the decision over. I was thrilled. "I would, and I already know one musician I want to bring with me."

"You name him. Anyone you want."

I gestured towards the bar, where tall, lanky, dark-skinned Butch was leaning over the bar trying to get the bartender's attention. "The bass player."

The club owner scowled. "That could be a problem. I hope to attract a certain class of clientele. You understand what I'm saying."

I was stunned. "He's the best bass player in town."

"Sorry, can't do it."

I was deeply offended by the owner's racism, but equally offended by his stupidity. How could he not want to have the best musicians in his house band? "If I can't bring him, I'm not interested," I politely said. To this day I regret being polite. I should've unleashed a string of invective that would've sent my mother to an early grave if she heard it.

In the end I decided against music as a career. I could be a journeyman musician, but lacked the talent to be more than that. True talent is innate. A musician needs to think in notes just as a mathematician thinks in numbers. I had the technique but lacked an intuitive feel for the infrastructure of music. A true jazz musician can hear a chord and know what notes it contains and how the notes will clash or mesh with other chords, can sense which way the chords will move, can hear harmonies and know how they are assembled, and on the spot and without deliberation, can weave all of this together into a compelling improvisation.

My decision was also based on a gradual realization as I recovered my physical strength and felt some distance from my family that I had more to my brain than music. As much as I loved music, it didn't satisfy my need to understand as much about life as I could. I was intellectually curious, a realization that came as something of a revelation to me who had until then felt like a dunce.

Near the end of my time at the Crosstown, I sat in with the Charlie Byrd Trio at Byrd's club, the Showboat Lounge. I had decided to go back to college, and this would be a nice way to end my musical career. I knew Byrd's bass player Keter Betts from jamming with him at Butch's house. I was scared but eager when invited to sit in.

Byrd, a balding man who looked like a kindly country doctor, played an amplified classical guitar without a pick. He called for blues in E flat and started to count off. I went through the agonies of the damned as I pondered the protocol of sitting in. I could handle blues in every key *except* E flat—B flat, F, G, no problem, just please not E flat. Did I have the right to ask him to choose another key? Or would that be an unforgivable sin for an invited guest? In the seconds between the counts of one and four, I decided it would be unprofessional to do anything other than suck it up, and the band started to play. My ruin came when it was my turn to improvise.

Oh, the pain, the agony. I stumbled so badly the bass player and drummer thought I was playing double-time, and being the superb musicians they were, they instantly doubled the beat, which knocked me even further off stride. They cooked, whereas I was like a drunk without a lamppost, and I lay in the gutter for what seemed like hours while passing cars splattered mud in my face. Ever since, I have been unable to listen to a Charlie Byrd CD without cringing.

—◊◊◊—

After huge, intimidating MIT, I wanted a small, personal college. Someone I knew from high school went to Trinity College and liked it, and that was good enough for me.

From the moment I set foot on the Trinity campus in Hartford, I was driven to prove to myself and to my father that I wasn't dumb. MIT had been a near-death experience, and I was determined not to repeat it. I studied like a man possessed, the polar opposite of my high school habits. I joined the debate team and dabbled in campus politics, but otherwise I studied. My roommate told me at year's end I had been an inspiration. My mid-term grades were lousy, but by the end of first semester, I was holding my own.

The cave in which I hid during high school was now matched by tunnel vision in college. In neither case could I see clearly. Fear drove both adaptations, but, damn, did I learn to study. My grades rose.

One day during second semester my English professor asked me to stay after class. I had not studied as thoroughly as usual and assumed I had flunked the test on Shakespeare which the professor had handed back to everyone except me. After the others left the room, he handed my test to me. To my astonishment, he had written A+ at the top. To my even greater astonishment, he told me that finding a student who could write as well as I was the kind of thing an English professor lived for. It had only happened two or three times in his teaching career, he said, and he urged me to major in English.

I didn't give his encouragement much credence, the idea too far-fetched for a young man raised in a pragmatic, get-ahead, success-must-be-measurable family. To tell the truth I thought the professor didn't know what he was talking about. I thanked him and promptly put the idea out of my mind.

I studied so hard at Trinity that I was a functional recluse, but I did well, and by the end of sophomore year, I sought a harder challenge. I applied to Yale and was one of four transfer students accepted that year. That should have been proof enough that I was smart, but by then my sights had risen. I sought tangible, irrefutable proof. My goal was to hold a Phi Beta Kappa key in my hand.

—◁◻▷—

In November of 1960, my sophomore year at Trinity, I drove to my grandmother's house in southern New Jersey for Thanksgiving dinner. The extended family had gathered there each Thanksgiving for as long as I could remember. Since Mother's late father had been an inventor, the house was equipped with now-commonplace but then out-of-the-ordinary conveniences such as central air conditioning. The house was a many roomed but compact Colonial on a sizeable but unostentatious lawn. Good taste prevailed.

Mother's parents had been the uncrowned royalty of Wenonah. Her father invented the machine which made corrugated boxes commercially viable and founded a company to manufacture his invention. His company made the family rich by small town standards, and both parents were civic-minded. Mother imbibed a sense of noblesse oblige from them. Do well by helping others. Do the right thing, don't seek credit. Warm heart, stiff upper lip.

The dining room seemed small with the uncles, aunts, and cousins crowded into it. Even with all the leaves in the mahogany table, the cousins, uncles, aunts, brothers and sisters could barely squeeze around it. People sat so close together that cutting meat became a test of finesse. Dede, my grandmother, owned the end of the table nearest the kitchen. She was a small, determined woman who got her way, thank you very much. There was no question who ran the house, but Dede was content to stay in the shadows letting others exercise their egos as long as she prevailed in the end.

Dad dominated the dinner table discussion, as he did at home—but my uncle Bryant brooked no nonsense. Bryant had taken over the family business when my grandfather died. He collected art and had a pilot's license (he and his wife Sue would die tragically nine years later in the crash of his plane). He had strong opinions and ate with lightning speed.

"I thought Nixon would win," Bryant said when he had finished his

Tony's maternal grandmother Jessica Langston (Dede)

turkey and dressing and Dede's signature cranberry sauce. "What happened?"

Dad filled his lungs. "Television."

"The first debate?"

"He refused makeup. He looked furtive and mean. You can't win elections like that, especially running against a charismatic guy like Kennedy."

"I voted for Kennedy, but for your sake I wish Nixon had won."

"Why on earth would anyone vote for Kennedy?"

"Nixon seems flawed to me," Bryant said.

Dad bristled. "Name someone who isn't flawed, as you put it."

I found Dad intimidating but Bryant didn't. "Most flawed people don't run for president."

Dad shifted in his chair. "I'm fed up with people psychoanalyzing Nixon. You have no idea what he went through."

Bryant didn't take the bait. "What will you do after you leave office in January, Bill?"

Dad hated it when someone wouldn't join him in argument. "Go back to private practice, I suppose. I haven't had time to think about it." Dad had briefly been with a law firm before he joined Tom Dewey in the New York District Attorney's office. "Really, Bryant, think before you join the chorus of Nixon haters. Everyone piles on when someone loses, but few have the guts to compete."

In the ensuing silence, I read the faces around the table. Everyone knew that Dad refused to lose arguments, but expressions varied from intimidated to blasé. Uncle Dick could care less, cousin Priscilla looked worried. The further from politics, the less intimidated the person. I loved these dinners.

After dinner, most of the family gathered in the living room. I joined Dale and Jeff on the sofa. We could overhear Mother telling Bryant and Dede that Dale was applying for a Woodrow Wilson Fellowship after Cornell.

"Is that true?" I quietly asked Dale.

"Yes."

"Wow."

"Don't wow me. I haven't gotten it yet."

"You will. You get everything you try for."

"I hear you're transferring."

"Maybe. I hope so."

Dale couldn't sit still any longer. "I'll be right back," she said, leaving Jeff and me on the sofa. I had been struck since arriving how mature Jeff seemed compared to a few months ago. Now in his junior year of high school, he was vice president of the student council, star halfback on

The Rogers brothers, c. 1966 (left to right) *Doug, Jeff, Tony*

the football team, and his science project had been selected to represent Sidwell at the D.C. Science Fair. "Congratulations on everything you're doing," I told him. "I hate you, but congratulations."

Jeff was competitive like Dad but less needy. "I'm not doing anything special."

"In this family, true. In any other family, you'd be the star."

Jeff shrugged. "I'm just doing what seems natural to me."

"Dad loves how well you're doing, I'll bet."

Jeff shrugged. "He likes football, that's why he comes."

"Wait a minute, Dad comes to your games?"

"Didn't he come to yours?"

"Are you kidding? I was only third-string. A waste of his time."

"It's not a big deal."

Dale returned. "Where's Doug?"

"I don't know," I said. "Hiding?"

"Being nice as usual," Jeff said.

Dale buzzed away to look for Doug. Jeff waited a second, then asked me, "What's college like?"

"All I do is study."

"Is it harder than high school?"

"Yes, by a lot. But once I got the hang of it, it's okay."

"Aren't you scared to transfer?"

I hadn't thought of it that way. "Not just about transferring. Before every exam, I want to throw up."

"How do you make yourself go through it?"

"I'm more scared by what will happen if I fail."

Jeff considered that. "Failure isn't an option in our family, is it?"

"I guess not, but how would you know? You ace everything you try."

"School and sports come naturally to me. I'm scared what will happen when I try something I'm not good at."

"You'll do fine. You make it look easy."

Jeff shook his head. "Wrong."

—⁂—

In order to understand the world better, I needed to know more of it. We had lived in Scarsdale before we moved to Bethesda, and Bethesda since then. Even insular me knew that neither was like the rest of the world.

From the age of sixteen I worked in the summer, in the D.C. public library shelving books, at a National Institute of Health research lab cleaning the cages of laboratory monkeys, and performing on the boat to Europe with the Rhythm Rockers. In college, I worked in different cities each summer. One summer I worked in the stock room of the Pacific Telephone and Telegraph company. I lived in Berkeley and took a bus across the Bay Bridge to work in San Francisco. Another summer I was a day camp counselor at a settlement house on the Near North Side of Chicago. I was in charge of a group of eight-and nine-year-old boys, most of whom had migrated north from Appalachia after their fathers lost work in the coal mines. The first day of camp, I was trying to herd my kids onto a chartered bus to go to the zoo. With my East

Coast, Ivy League manners, I politely suggested the kids might want to get on the bus. "Okay, guys, this will be fun. You'll have a good time. Really." Nothing. I escalated from suggesting to urging. "Get on the bus, guys. Let's go." No luck. Desperation, abject failure on my first day. Begging, perhaps? "Please, guys, we don't want to be last on the bus, do we?"

I felt someone tugging on my pants leg. Irritated, I looked down. It was one of my nine year olds. "Tony," he said. "Sometimes you have to yell."

I did. "Okay, guys! GET ON THE BUS!"

It worked.

CHAPTER NINE

Plato

AT YALE I STARTED seriously thinking about what I wanted to do after college. Having eliminated engineering and music, and dismissed out-of-hand my professor's suggestion of pursuing writing, I had no career aspirations. People often stayed with one employer their whole lifetimes, unlike now where loyalty to or from an employer is unusual, so the initial choice fresh out of college had deep significance. I thought of politics. How better to honor my father while besting him? But that assumed I could best him, difficult to do when your father has been a cabinet officer. Anyway I had the wrong personality for politics (though I suppose if a recluse like Richard Nixon could do it, so could a recluse named Tony Rogers). Law was the family business but it didn't interest me, so I didn't know what I wanted to do.

Except go to New York City almost every weekend to see Miles Davis and John Coltrane and the other musicians I loved. I stayed with a family friend who had an apartment on 14th Street and was also a jazz lover. He and I, and sometimes just me, frequented the Village Vanguard, Birdland, and the other now legendary jazz clubs. What an incredible musical era I grew up in. Rock and roll and I came of age at the same time, rhythm and blues and Motown were in full swing, the jazz of the late fifties and early sixties has never been bettered, and Dylan and the Beatles were on the near horizon. I didn't see Dylan in his Greenwich Village days, to my regret, but did see him in Worcester, Massachusetts, shortly after he went electric. I saw Aretha Franklin at a bar in Philly before the Muscle Shoals sessions, when she was known primarily as a jazz piano player and singer, and later live in concert in Paris after she became a soul legend. I once took a blind date to a college dance at which the Count Basie Orchestra was playing. It was our first and last date since I barely spoke to her. Instead I stood a few feet in front of the bandstand soaking up the power of a big band in full swing and mesmerized by how the unamplified guitar of Freddie Greene could anchor the entire rhythm section.

I didn't make many friends at Yale. Partly because I entered in my junior year, after my classmates had formed friendships, partly because transferring halfway through college set me back academically at first. Yale was more intimidating than Trinity, with large lecture classes and professors with impressive reputations. My grades were good, but not stellar. I feared I had made a mistake. To make up for lost momentum, I studied even harder. Other than going to dinner in the Davenport dining room (where we had to wear ties), and to New York many weekends, I stayed in my room and studied. Even with non-stop studying, my goal of making Phi Beta Kappa seemed out of reach.

Funny how raising one's goal can hurt one's confidence. I had started college with the goal of proving I was smart. By transferring to Yale, I had proved that by any objective standard, but now I felt that if I didn't someday hold a Phi Beta Kappa key in my hand, it would prove my original assessment was true. My freshman counselor at Trinity, when I bemoaned my inability to do college work, had warned me that if I studied harder than I thought humanly possible, I could eventually reach a point where I was doing very well, but if I wanted to do better than that, if I wanted to do *really well*, I would have to find it in me to study even harder. If you reach that point, you will have to make a conscious decision, he told me. I had reached that point, and decided to go for it.

Most of my senior year courses were elective and I elected to take a one semester seminar on Plato's *Republic*, taught by Allan Bloom. I had never taken a semester course devoted to one book. Philosophy appealed to me, but the introductory course I had taken the year before bored me to tears. How do we know a table is a table? We don't, now get on with it. How to live and what does it all mean, I wanted to know.

There were eight or nine of us in the seminar. Allan Bloom was in his thirties, but seemed much older to me. Tall when he stood straight, which he rarely did, being perpetually hunched over as if searching for an idea he had dropped, ashes from his cigarette painting his shirt like a pointillist, he came across as a person who never thought about the impression he made. In the political world I had been raised in, impressions could make or break a career. Surfaces were more important that substance. Bloom seemed oblivious to surfaces.

By making connections between lines of dialogue that seemed to have no connection, Professor Bloom taught us to think about what Plato intended, not about what he said. That was his method, which he had learned from Leo Strauss, a legendary/notorious University of Chicago professor I hadn't heard of before. There were no quizzes, no tests, only rigorous analysis in class and an occasional long paper. The final grade was based on classroom participation and the papers.

I remember one paper I wrote in which, following Bloom's method, I arrived at philosophical insights which startled me because they were original with me, not found anywhere in the dialogues. I remember feeling almost an electric shock as I wrote the paper. I could connect ideas, draw conclusions. I turned in the paper with trepidation. It's one thing to be able to think, another to be right, and I worried my conclusions were way off base.

Professor Bloom met with each of us privately after we turned in papers. He met with me in the seminar room. The A+ he had written at the top of the paper called to mind the shock of seeing the A+ my English professor at Trinity had given me. But what Professor Bloom said about my paper is what really stunned me. He said, "I've never read anything better at the undergraduate level." Unlike the English test where I felt unprepared, therefore undeserving of my professor's praise,

I had sweated over this paper. To have one of the smartest men I had ever met say that about my paper was head turning.

I was now one of Bloom's anointed. He fancied himself a modern day Socrates and gathered a handful of his favorite students in his apartment once a week for non-credit seminars. Imagine, to be among the chosen! Our topic was Shakespeare (speaking of hidden connections, what was the subject of the exam which led to my English professor urging me to write?). We literally sat at Bloom's feet, there not being enough chairs for everyone in his small apartment. In Allan Bloom's world, brains were everything. Imagine what it felt like for a former dummy like me to be there. Like being knighted. Like winning a beauty pageant after an adolescence of being told you are too fat or too skinny. Like being named first-string quarterback on your high school football team and throwing the deciding touchdown in the last ten seconds of the most important game of the season.

I'm not sure when my misgivings about Professor Bloom began, sometime in the first weeks of the second semester, I suppose. We studied Rousseau's *Social Contract* the second semester. I found Rousseau to be nowhere near the rigorous thinker that Plato was and somewhat of a bore, and I began to get a creepy feeling about Professor Bloom's intellectual salon. Being among the chosen took on a slightly sinister connotation. Independent thinking among the chosen was strongly encouraged, but one was expected to ultimately agree with the master. To put it another way, the impression Bloom gave was that rigorous independent analysis would always lead to agreement with him. The only reasons anyone wouldn't agree with him (and his master, Leo Strauss) were because (1) they hadn't rigorously thought about the problem, or (2) they were stupid.

For me, who had felt dumb until Bloom anointed me, the choice became to break with him and feel dumb again, or stay loyal and remain smart. I didn't realize until later that this was his method: he spotted smart young men with inferiority complexes and gained their allegiance by making them feel brilliant (several of his acolytes went on to become the neo-cons of the George W. Bush administration).

Graduation from Yale, 1963

There were additional reasons for my growing disenchantment with Professor Bloom. By the end of the seminar on *The Republic*, I realized that he believed literally in Socrates's concept of philosopher-king. Democracy to Socrates and to Professor Bloom meant law and order under the rule of the smartest men in a society. That wasn't my definition of democracy. I was being taught by a would-be philosopher-king, and I didn't like it. The other half of the creepy feeling was a growing awareness that there was something sexual in the air during Bloom's apartment seminars. Socrates had loved boys, after all.

Bloom, being smart, sensed my disenchantment, and took me aside one evening to say that if I wanted to break with him, he could understand, but pleaded with me not to turn my back on philosophy. He urged me to study philosophy in graduate school.

Unlike my English professor urging me to write, which was too far removed from my pragmatic upbringing to take seriously, I took Bloom's recommendation very seriously. Classically, until perhaps Kant, philosophy had addressed the big questions I had thought about since I began to think for myself. Too often the current philosophy dissolved into an in-group, group-grope type of debate to which outsiders were not invited. I liked abstract thinking but not brain games. I wanted my thinking to be tethered to reality at some level. I was no longer the young man who rejected a suggestion to study literature because it seemed impractical and slightly nutty, but I still wanted what I studied to give me insight into the world and its meaning (big mistake say today's philosophers: meaning has no meaning. Then why study philosophy? I ask).

Which still left the question, what to do after graduation? I could get a graduate degree and teach, I suppose, but teaching had never appealed to me. Politics, engineering, music, and literature I had ruled out, and had never for a moment considered business or medicine. Which left law. I still had no desire to practice law, but law was in my family's DNA and kept popping up when I ran out of other ideas. I rationalized that a law degree would open the door to a whole bunch of possibilities besides law, and that law and philosophy bear some relation to each other.

I told Professor Bloom of my plans. He took them well, telling me that he could see me on the Supreme Court someday. He gave me an A+ for the course, even though my work on Rousseau was subpar. I applied to Harvard Law School and was accepted.

I finished college feeling let down and uncertain. Warnings should be given to entering freshman: beware of your final semester. The emphasis in high school on getting into a good college, and the pressure, self-imposed and otherwise, to get good grades in college, all lead to a massive letdown when you come face-to-face with the rest of your life. Are you telling me that life continues after college? Is that what you're telling me?

I graduated magna cum laude but hadn't made Phi Beta Kappa. I didn't know what to think. Some students had been selected on the basis of grades before the final semester, but I hadn't made the cut. Final grades would be factored into the next round, with results announced sometime during the summer.

CHAPTER TEN

Mowing

GETTING INTO HARVARD Law School should have pleased Dad but if it did, I didn't feel it. As I saw it, Dad only took note of failure. Probably not true. What was true was that Dad seemed more afraid of failure than proud of success. Once failure was averted, success seemed a given. I had by now lived through enough successes and failures to spot an insecure man when I saw one.

I lived at home that summer and worked on a farm in Potomac, Maryland. The farm grew sod for golf courses and hotels. I learned about the farm from a high school friend who had worked there, and took the job because I had never done physical labor of any kind and wanted to try it. For ten hours a day, I cleaned barns and did farm chores, but mostly I drove an American Harvester tractor pulling a low-to-the-ground disc mower which trimmed the grass to golf course height. I felt more like a barber than a farmer.

The fields were not contiguous. To get to the field I was mowing for the day I had to drive my tractor on county roads. Commuters fumed when they were stuck behind me, but tractors were not uncommon on the roads at the time (they would be unthinkable in Potomac now). Whenever I passed another tractor, I would tip my hat and feel special.

Working in the Maryland sun all day gave new meaning to the word hot. I had never experienced anything like it, even though I had lived through a dozen un-air-conditioned Washington summers. I wore a hat the size of a disc on a roller harrow to keep the sun off my face, and long sleeves to keep it off my arms. The heat lifted the smells of the sod and soil off the ground, where they took up permanent residence in my nose. When I got home at the end of the day, I showered on the second floor then went up to my room on the third floor, only to be felled by heat once more. The box fan in the bedside window succeeded only in rearranging the humidity. I never cooled off that summer, but I did get used to the heat.

It was a summer in which I should have been able to look back at college and feel good about what I had accomplished. That never happened, because as soon as I graduated the bottom fell out of the cave where I had taken refuge in my early teens. Everything I had taken for granted, who I was and my place in the world, the self-evident truths I had accepted without thought, vanished overnight, leaving a void. Annihilation of the self is the ultimate loneliness.

The irony. My hiding place had served me well through my teens and into my twenties, had preserved enough of my DNA through the vicissitudes of father and college to reconstruct myself when the coast was clear. The coast now being clear, my cave collapses, and I am lost. Fate, you sadist.

In addition to endless mowing, I plowed fields after the sod had been harvested. A specialized machine driven by another farmhand cut a lateral slice beneath the grass, then rolled up the soil to be trucked away to hotels and golf courses.

I enjoyed plowing more than mowing. Neither required much thought, only the ability to drive in a straight line, leaving me plenty of time to panic. I had known that identity was fungible, but hadn't realized that all semblance of it could be lost. I had no idea where to look for myself because I no longer knew who to look for.

The family house provided a measure of safety. The same house where for years I had no safe place except a bathroom. Maybe it felt safe now because nothing in it seemed familiar, even my parents. And the fact I

On the tractor at Pearson's farm, Potomac, Maryland, summer 1963

didn't know who I was, so wasn't worried about Dad bending me out of shape.

My ham radio still stood on the table by the door, but I had no urge to talk to anyone, no urge to contact the few people I knew from college and high school who might be in town for the summer. I lacked the energy, the motivation. I attributed it to the heat.

In the heat and isolation, I turned to books. I had long been an avid magazine reader and had devoured comic books when a boy, but I wasn't in the habit of reading books for pleasure. Steinbeck's *Travels with Charley* was in the house (undoubtably my mother's since Dad didn't read books that weren't about current events). I took it up to my room and started reading. The book appealed to someone who wanted to learn more about the world and how the people in it lived. I loved Steinbeck's plain and simple prose, his honesty, his humanity. I looked forward to reading it at night when I got home from work. Timing is everything in life, and the book may have sunk in because my defenses were shot, but I had found an author who spoke to me. I hadn't realized how deeply a book could stir the soul. A Yale, Trinity, and Sidwell Friends education hadn't done that. It took reading John Steinbeck in a sweltering room.

Driving a tractor is hypnotic, especially in the hot sun. The muffled roar, the huge tires slowly revolving, the weight of the mower felt in the seat of my pants even though the tractor was doing the work. It's especially trance-like when all one can see is grass in every direction. How could I regain my personality? was the question for many days of trance-filled hours. I tried at first to re-erect what I thought of as my identity, but the scaffolding was beyond repair. Stripped of one's defenses, the habitual comes to seem abnormal. The incessant bobbing and weaving I had done to fend off Dad's criticism, the taking on of protective coloring, now seemed repellent. Anyway (as I thought the problem through) I hadn't been all that fond of myself growing up. I had considered myself unlikeable. Fundamentally flawed. Guilty of some horrible, unnamed wrong. Why re-constitute that person? On the other hand (why oh why is there always an 'on the other hand' in life?) the way forward seemed like night, and I had no idea how to get where I wanted to go, if I knew where I wanted to go. To move forward in total darkness was to risk never finding my way back. What I had was a dilemma, a quandary, laughable if it didn't hurt so much.

One afternoon of scorching heat my tractor broke down in a field far from the farm. I climbed down to look for a house where I might use the phone. None were visible so I walked to the edge of the field and started down the road. I came to a rundown shack of a house a quarter-mile away and knocked on the screen door. The door hung loosely on its hinges and rattled when I knocked. After a few moments, a bedraggled young woman in a halter top came to the door. "Yes?" she asked through the screen.

"Do you have a phone I could use? I'm mowing a field down the road and my tractor broke. I need to call my boss."

She opened the screen door and looked me over. "Sure, come in. Don't wake the baby."

I followed her into the dark house. No lights were on, and little sun got through the windows. "In here," she said.

She showed me the phone. "Thanks," I said.

I dialed my boss' number and waited. While I waited, I noticed something pale lying on the sofa. A doll? It moved a little. Not a doll, a dog? A cat? Whatever it was was covered with flies. I took a closer look and recoiled when I realized I was looking at a baby.

My boss answered the phone and said he was on his way. He'd meet me at the tractor.

I hung up and stood where I was, taking in the shabbiness, the darkness of the room. The furniture looked sledge-hammered. I felt sick. This, less than twenty miles from Our Nation's Capitol. Should I say something to the young mother? Something like, get the goddamn flies off your baby? "Thanks," I mumbled on my way out and walked down the road to the waiting tractor.

I felt flattened when I wasn't on the job, but the rhythm of days on the tractor boosted my mood just high enough to see a little ahead. I couldn't believe I would be starting law school in September. I was neither scared nor enthusiastic. It had gotten Dad off my back, for which I was grateful. Dale was studying for her PhD in Political Science at Berkeley, Jeff was a counselor at a summer camp, and Doug kept out of sight. I went to my room every night and read. What I read seemed more real than the house but less real than the fields.

Toward the end of summer, I mowed a field north of any I had mowed before. To get to it I had to pass a strip mall and cross a busy highway. Perched on my tractor wearing my wide-brimmed straw hat, I felt anachronistic and arrived at the field to find a long, rolling expanse of grass that provided much longer views than I was used to. I idled my tractor for a moment to look west; the horizon! I could see the horizon! Sounds silly to get enthusiastic about such a simple thing, but the sightlines in and around Washington, D.C., are not expansive. Smiling inside but probably not openly, I put the tractor in gear and rolled forward.

The humidity had dried to an extent, although everything is relative. The air felt clean, if not crisp. I clipped the grass to the exact height my boss demanded, proud of my precision, my morning's work proof that I had learned a lot that summer.

At noon, I parked my tractor at the base of a small rise and sat down on top to eat my lunch. I made himself a sandwich everyday before leaving for work, usually peanut butter and jelly, which in high humidity tasted like sawdust but today tasted pretty good. When I finished the sandwich, I realized I had been staring into the distance while I ate. How can the mind so abstract itself to be unaware of what one is seeing, of the passage of time? Where does the mind go? Is self-awareness necessary to be one's self?

The field contained swells that looked hypnotic from the rise. Rhythm again; a Native American artist once wrote, "He who controls rhythm, controls." I felt something stirring inside. Up popped the dilemma I had tabled at the beginning of summer. Whether to try to reconstruct my former self or move forward in the dark, a stranger to myself. The latter scared me more than Dad. I wondered how the mentally ill hung on; to be sick in the soul, to have one's very self be sick, must be terrifying.

Turning points come unannounced. As I stared abstractly at the horizon, depressed and frightened, I felt something I had never felt before. I didn't know what to name it. A swelling. Not sex, not anything so simple. No, something new, some urge to take a scene like the one I was looking at and recreate it to pay homage, to understand it. To look at a different angle, to see it more clearly. To build (my engineering urge, again!), to imagine into existence, to know.

Turning points not only come unannounced, they are often unacknowledged until later, if ever. I had no idea I had reached a fulcrum of my life (how often such moments occur when one has almost given up hope), no idea until much later. All I knew at the time was that I felt something I hadn't felt before, and all I knew for several years was that my vision on the rise stuck with me. But the immediate choice was whether to move forward in the dark and risk never encountering myself again. Yes.

Yes. The choice I made was yes. But to move forward does not mean to be well. I entered law school feeling only half there. Good luck getting through Harvard Law School on half a brain, I told myself.

CHAPTER ELEVEN

Heartland

My FIRST IMPRESSION of Harvard Law School was how smart everyone was, students and faculty alike. It was daunting. Classes, for the most part, were held in large lecture halls with assigned seats. The professors had seating charts and called on students by name. "Mr. Rogers, please state the facts in *U.S. v Blowhard.*" Woe unto thee if unprepared. The faculty was demanding but not cruel as legend would have it. Students were challenged if they made a poorly reasoned argument—this was, after all, a professional school, not Little League—but the professors did not try to cut a student off at the knees. The pressure on us was largely self-imposed: to escape humiliation in front of our classmates. To answer a professor's question with "unprepared, sir," was to place oneself in stocks on the village square for days.

Classes were taught using the Socratic method, which meant reading case after case after case. We studied the building blocks of law—contracts, property, taxes. The amount of reading was prodigious. We weren't taught The Law, we were taught how to reason our way to the law by extracting a precedent from past cases and applying it to a newly presented set of facts. By doing this time after time, we reached an understanding of the guiding principles of the law. In a way it did not differ significantly from Allan Bloom's method of teaching.

I lived on the third floor of a three-family house in an apartment I shared with another student. I'm afraid I wasn't great company. I was acutely aware of how impaired my brain was, and I struggled just to keep up with the case load.

One of my earliest discoveries about law school colored the rest of my time there. "To think like a lawyer" meant to deliberately drain emotion from one's thinking. Makes sense if the goal is impartial justice—we are, after all, a nation of laws, not emotion — but it makes for dull reading and reasoning. I hadn't realized until then how much I prized emotion, how basic it was to my conception of being human. But the existential crisis that began at the tail end of college and lasted through the long summer had shut me down emotionally. I felt cut off from people, I couldn't reach them and they couldn't reach me. I had dated a girl in college but the changes I was going through had soured her on me. I can't blame her; I wouldn't have dated me, either.

Early in the semester I climbed the stairs to our apartment after Real Property, feeling overwhelmed. My roommate had been there earlier and put the mail on the kitchen table. A thick envelope from Yale caught my attention. I opened it thinking they had caught on to my tricks and were rescinding my degree.

I found a letter inside. When I opened it, a metal something fell out and onto the floor. I leaned down and picked it up. A key of some sort.

I looked closely. A Phi Beta Kappa key.

I couldn't make sense of what I saw in my hand. If I had made Phi Beta Kappa, why the delay?

"It is my pleasure to inform you that you have been elected to Phi Beta Kappa." The letter explained that the second round of voting, which is held after final grades are in, had been delayed that year due to unforeseen circumstances. "Congratulations," the letter ended, "and welcome to Phi Beta Kappa."

I had expected elation if this moment ever came, but what I felt was disgust. I had worked my ass off for *this*? A fucking key? Suddenly grades seemed meaningless; worse, they seemed corrupt, venal.

I ran down the stairs to the backyard, tore the cover off the garbage

Tony, 1964

can and threw the key into the can.

Wasted years chasing grades. Empty achievement. Good riddance. I went back upstairs and washed my hands.

I slept soundly that night, feeling cleansed. I awoke the next morning in panic.

What had I done? I raced downstairs praying that the garbage truck hadn't come. I was in luck. I carried the key upstairs and put it in a safe place.

—∞—

I knew halfway through first year that the law wasn't for me, so the question was, should I drop out? Two and a half more years of learning stuff I probably wouldn't put to use professionally seemed a form of self-flagellation, yet I decided to stick it out. I'm not sure why. There was a certain amount of pride involved. I couldn't imagine a tougher intellectual challenge than to get through Harvard Law School, and I wanted to prove I could do it. Practicality also entered into it, a Harvard Law degree would be a good credential to have. Last but not least, my parents were paying the tuition and dropping out would bitterly disappoint them.

Yet I persist in thinking, even after all these years, that the reasons I stayed in law school were mainly psychological: to finish what I had started for a change, to not be the quitter my anonymous erstwhile fraternity brother had accused me of being, and, yes, to do what my father had done, only better (Harvard beats Cornell, doesn't it?). The ironies continue to pile up—for psychological reasons I stayed at a school that eschewed psychology and emotion.

The grade in most courses was based solely on the final exam. For year-long courses, you didn't know how you were doing until after the course was over and the final exam taken. An exception was made for first year students, who took a non-credit midyear exam to give us some idea if we were sinking or swimming. I was doing neither, I was treading water. Good enough for someone who had already decided against law as a career.

Since everything depends on the final exam, the pressure at exam time is intense. A probably apocryphal story circulated from the day we enrolled of a student who cracked under the pressure and disappeared, only to be discovered by his roommates twenty-four hours later standing under the hot shower where he had been the whole time. His skin, according to the story, resembled a prune. Non-apocryphal students were known to prop their case books open on the glass shelves above the sink and study while they shaved or brushed their teeth. The cavernous law library, where we all spent countless hours all year, became a place of sweat and the smell of fear in the weeks before exams. I did okay on the exams. Not great, but okay. We were graded to the one-hundredths of a point: 3.15, 3.22, 3.56, etc., and our ranks in class posted for all to see. I was slightly below the middle. Given that I had been functioning on half a brain all year, the ranking seemed apt.

Heaving a sigh of relief at surviving, and knowing that the odds of getting through the rest of law school intact were now in my favor, I did what all diligent first year law students do for the summer: I drove to the Midwest and looked for work on a farm. Of course most students do nothing of the sort, they intern in law firms, but since I wasn't going to practice law, I felt free to do what I wanted. And what I wanted was to finish the thinking process I had started on the sod farm the summer before. A tractor was a good place to do it.

I had long been fascinated by the concept of America's heartland, and working there strongly appealed to me. See the core of America, its center. And I wanted to test how I would fare without a plan. So much of my life had been programmed. If you grow up in a prosperous suburb, go to a private school, and your parents are educated and successful, you do X, Y, and Z. I wanted to see how I would handle an unfamiliar alphabet.

What I did was drive west looking for fields I'd like to work. My initial thought was Kansas, which I assumed was flat throughout. Flat appealed to me precisely because I had grown up in rolling. I drove through Southern Illinois which to my surprise was completely, utterly flat (a new sensation standing by the side of the road in flat, flat land— the earth a stage on which anything vertical becomes the lead actor), on through the landscape of Missouri (rolling but more like swells than waves), and into Kansas. Which to my disappointment was not flat, at least not immediately west of Kansas City. I drove on until I reached the pancake-flat part of Kansas, but decided I liked the landscape of Missouri better and retraced my steps. Halfway across Missouri, at the midpoint between Kansas City and St. Louis, I found landscape that appealed to me as neither too flat nor too rolling, but just right, and I stopped at a farm and asked for work.

He didn't have anything but knew a farmer down the road who might. Herman Knipp's son had left the farm to try his luck in Chicago, and Knipp was looking for a farmhand. "Down the road a mile. You'll see a long driveway on the left. Can't miss it."

I thanked him. We had been standing by a wooden fence and a field lying fallow. The smell of soil and growing things was overpowering. No doubt who is the boss in farm country.

Corn lined the road to Knipp's farm, punctuated by fields of soybeans. Sometimes I couldn't see past the corn, other times I could see the distant horizon.

The driveway to Knipp's farm appeared. I couldn't miss it, as the man had said. I approached the farmhouse cautiously, my tires kicking up dust. To the right of the farmhouse were a small barn and silo. I caught glimpses of a bigger barn and other outbuildings beyond the house.

I pulled the parking brake. A stout woman answered the door.

"Herman's not here. You'll find him in the soybeans, over there." She pointed beyond the farm buildings.

"He won't mind being interrupted?"

"You won't be able to tell. He doesn't give much away."

"Thanks."

Knipp was wearing overalls and a plaid longsleeve shirt. A man in his sixties, solid, going bald I saw when we kneeled down and he took off his hat.

He wiped his brow with his sleeve.

"Your neighbor told me you might be looking for a hand."

Knipp waited. "Could be. You ever worked on a farm?"

"Yes. Last summer in Maryland. We grew sod."

Knipp's eyes searched for a piece of straw, which he put between his teeth. "Sod?"

"For hotels, golf courses."

Knipp had a broad face, an ample billboard for emotions, but he chose not to display any. "Know how to drive a tractor?"

"Yes, sir. That's mostly what I did."

Knipp stirred the dust with the piece of straw and stuck it back between his teeth. We were kneeling and my knees began to ache. "You said last summer. What do you do the rest of the year?"

"Go to law school."

Knipp thought a long time after hearing that. You could see him rearranging his mental files whenever he absorbed a new fact. "Where?"

"Harvard."

"Good school."

"Yes, sir."

"I tend seven hundred acres, by myself since my son left. Corn, soybeans, wheat, hogs, and a few head of cattle. No slacking off, arrive on time. Work until the work is done."

"Sounds good to me."

"You'll go back to school at the end of summer?"

"Yes, sir."

"Gives me the summer to look for a permanent hand. When can you start?"

"Tomorrow."

"Eight a.m."

We discussed where I might live. He and his wife had a spare room but couldn't put me up because she was in poor health. "There's one hotel in town." He told me how to get there.

To get there, I drove back the way I came on two lane Highway 50 (50 Highway as they say out there) and took a right at a small road sign indicating Tipton. I passed a few neat rows of streets lined with houses, then came to a main street. Scanning the street, I could see a Rexall drugstore, a Chevrolet dealer, a café, and a cluster of small stores. I turned right, as Herman Knipp had told me to do, and came to the rickety hotel, three stories of clapboard siding with an ancient wooden fire escape much too big for the hotel. As if they had built the fire escape first and used up most of the wood.

I took a room. They had plenty. My room had a kitchenette and a bathroom with a tin shower stall. I couldn't take a shower in it without clanging my elbows against the metal. I sounded like a bad steel band.

I unpacked the few things I had brought with me and succumbed to loneliness for the first time since I started on my journey. Whoa! How was I going to make it through the summer? I sat on the bed which sagged when I sat, the springs the kind you find on summer camp cots. Collect your thoughts, Tony. You are here and you are okay.

I left the hotel to explore the town, which didn't take long. I liked the feel of the main drag. Railroad tracks cut through town behind the stores on the street—street, stores, track. A train station and a grain silo anchored the line of stores. The town fit the definition of middle of nowhere as well as any, but it had context, and context lessened the lonely feeling. One got the distinct sense of fields lying just beyond the town even when you couldn't see them, and the sense impression was true I found when I crossed the railroad tracks and walked to the north edge of town. Three or four blocks of houses, then nothing but fields. A stark delineation, no dribbling out of houses and gas stations like you find at the edges of a suburb. I stood for a moment looking north, then retraced my steps through town until I came to 50 Highway on the southern side. Beyond that more fields. A town surrounded by fields. A farm town in farm country. Good fences make good neighbors, clear borders lend clear identity.

I was in the heartland.

CHAPTER TWELVE

Plowing

I DROVE JOHN DEERES that summer, big green tractors that pulled heavy plows and took no grief from anyone. Giant tractors possess awesome power but are slow to stop and hard to steer in a straight line, especially on rutted soil. Tractors are dictators. Tractors are temperamental. I heard of a young farmhand who was crushed by the tractor he was driving after it reared up on its gigantic rear tires and flung him to the ground.

I found driving a tractor on a Midwestern farm to be entirely different than driving a tractor on a Maryland sod farm. For one thing, I was plowing crops not mowing grass. For another, the vistas were much more expansive. One of Knipp's fields bordered the railroad tracks, and I could spot a train approaching from miles and miles away, only a glint of sun off its headlight at first, then a black shadow, then a ground shaking behemoth. If I was near the track when a train passed, the engineer would often tip his hat or give a wave.

I got a childish pleasure out of driving beside the track as a train passed. Sometimes I would be going in the opposite direction, which induced a sense of vertigo, sometimes I would futilely race the train. Either way was fun.

I was a little surprised to find that the sense of dread I had felt when the scaffolding under my personality collapsed the previous summer had not abated. The demands of law school had distracted me, but there was nothing to distract me here. I would plow a row of corn, get to the end, turn around, and head back. Row after row after row. One field could easily take a day to plow. Plenty of time to think.

I decided to do a Descartes. Scrap everything I had believed and start over.

Too bad Descartes didn't drive a tractor. The muffled roar of the engine, the rows of corn waiting patiently to be plowed, the relentless sun, allowed the mind to roam.

First things first. Strip yourself of everything that ties you to your old thinking. Steering with one hand, I removed my watch and stuffed it in my pocket. I would tell time by the sun. Now sweep your mind clean of what you learned from your father, the need to get ahead, to turn everything into a competition, concepts I had fought bitterly while growing up but which had imprinted me. Next, abandon everything you have learned since you started thinking for yourself, your defensiveness, your stunted aspirations. Start over. What do you consider important? Build a belief structure from the ground up.

What was the most fundamental human drive? That was easy. Working the land I saw how fervently all living things cling to life. Baby rabbits darting between rows of corn to escape circling hawks, hogs refusing to climb the chute into a truck that would take them to slaughter (they didn't rebel when I herded them into a truck to take them to the county fair, somehow they knew the difference), the hard work of farming to grow food so people can survive. The drive to stay alive. At root, all living creatures will do everything they can to survive.

Number two? That also was easy. Procreation. I did not need to study animals to discover the procreative drive, but working the land brought it into stark relief. There was something sensual about plowing the land under a hot sun.

Okay, survival and procreation. Numbers one and two.

From then on it got harder. Granted that a desire to survive and pro-create is built into our very genes, but to what purpose? We have higher parts of the brain and spirit that must be fulfilled, I firmly believed. We are animals and share many of the basic needs of other animals, but we also have a need for meaning and purpose. A spiritual side—does any other species practice religion? A creative side—does any other species make art? Survival and procreation may be bedrock, but what to build on the bedrock to satisfy our need for meaning is a question that has vexed human beings since the beginning. I would need more than a summer to think that through.

—⁂—

The porch was a gathering place for the old timers who lived in the hotel. Former farmers who had sold their farms and moved into the hotel rocked the long evenings away in the high-backed wooden rockers that stood at attention on the front porch. The porch wrapped around the front of the hotel, affording the men an uninterrupted view of the comings and goings about town. Or the absence thereof, there being little going on after dark. But darkness came late after a long prairie day, so there was plenty of time to watch for stragglers.

I wondered if I had the right to join the old timers on the porch. Not gregarious under the best of circumstances, I felt doubly uncomfortable out here—me, an effete Easterner, sitting down among grizzled men who had worked the land their whole lives. What drove me to sit was the loneliness of not knowing a soul, of listening to the soft twilight sounds and wishing I could share them with someone—the everyday loneliness that I rarely felt at home because I had walled myself off so completely.

"Okay if I join you?" I asked at the end of the row.

There were six men on the porch that night. "Sure. Take a seat."

Silent rocking. "Name's Carl Owens. Won't introduce you to the rest of the gang because you won't remember their names." The others nodded or gave a wave.

"Hi. Tony Rogers."

"Working for Herman, are you?"

"That's right."

"You came along just in time. He needed a hand to replace his son."

"He told me."

"Here for good?"

"No. The summer." I had debated how frank to be about what I did. Harvard Law School sounded alien out here. "I'm a law student."

"Oh?" Carl seemed amused. "Where?"

"Harvard."

The men rocked. "No kidding," Carl said, without inflection.

"No kidding."

Carl looked down the row of chairs. "You boys got anybody you want to sue?"

Chuckles. The man at the far end had his feet propped on the porch railing. "The United States government. My social security check was late this month."

Laughter. A man sitting in the middle said, "James, you have so much money you don't need a government check. Remind us, how much did you sell your farm for?"

"A lot more than you got for yours, Fred."

Hilarity. Carl turned to me. "Don't mind the boys. They got nothing else to do except try to be funny." He looked down the row. "Which they're not very good at."

From then on, I joined the men on the porch most evenings. Little was said, little was needed. The rocking was enough.

—⚮—

The loneliness of knowing you are a very small person in a very big universe is a useful loneliness. Not knowing anyone other than widowers and pensioners three times your age is a debilitating loneliness. When the rocking chair gang was not on the porch, I clung to the middle-aged desk clerk for companionship. The poor fellow wanted nothing more than to be left alone, and I wouldn't oblige. Thus it was a relief for both of us when I met a young man my age who taught music at the regional high school. Ralph and I had little in common except our ages and music, but that was plenty. His family was from Kansas City, and he drove the two and a half hours to the city most summer weekends. After I got to know him, he sometimes took me along.

Occasionally we would eat dinner together at one of the two eating places in town: the Tipton Café on Main Street, or the 50 Highway Bar and Grill outside of town. If we wanted variety, we drove west past fifteen miles of farmland to a bigger small town or twelve miles east to an itty-bitty town (which had the area's only movie theater).

The 50 Highway Bar and Grill was depressing in the extreme, dank, rarely busy, the smell of stale beer embedded in its DNA; I took myself there whenever I was feeling sorry for myself and got drunk on 3.2 beer while listening to Ray Charles on the jukebox.

The Tipton Café on the main drag was brighter and less hopeless, and had the advantage of a very pretty young waitress named Sheila. I was not usually shy around women, but she spooked me. Eating there with Ralph helped. They were acquainted.

"Do you think she notices me?" I asked Ralph one evening.

"Forget it. She's got a boyfriend."

"I was going to ask you to introduce me."

"She's wild. Even if she didn't have a boyfriend, I'd stay away from her."

"Really?"

"Her father threatened to shoot her last boyfriend."

"Really?"

"Stop saying 'really.' I double-dated with Sheila once. She and her boyfriend rode in the backseat and didn't say much. After a while I looked in the rearview mirror and saw why. Sheila was giving her boyfriend a blowjob."

I am grateful to Sheila. For the rest of the summer, every time she brought me my pork chops or Salisbury steak, I visualized her giving her boyfriend a blowjob in the backseat of Ralph's car.

—⁂—

Ralph and I stayed at his family's house when we went to Kansas City. I liked Kansas City, it had a companionable feel to it. Ralph's father ran a funeral home there. The family lived above it. The first time I visited, we entered through the funeral home and on the way to the stairs passed the body of a fourteen year old girl who had been electrocuted while watering her lawn. Ralph barely noticed. Only when he saw me turn white did he comment.

"Sorry. It's second nature to me. You've never seen a dead person before?"

"At a funeral, yes. On a gurney at a friend's house, no."

There were no dead bodies in my hotel room, at least as far as I knew, but it was home base for a battalion of cockroaches. Outnumbering me by the hundreds, they took little note of my presence, reconnoitering every night on the floor beneath my bed. The bed, thank god, had metal legs, which apparently they couldn't climb since none made it up to where I slept. If I needed to go the bathroom at night, I had to turn on the light and give them time to scurry away, otherwise I'd step on a platoon of them. It was a weird sight: for an instant after I turned on the light, I'd see a solidly black floor, then the light would spur the cockroach army into action, and they would scatter away, making pissed-off scratching sounds with their legs. I became inured to it, as long as the roaches observed the demilitarized zone that was my mattress.

In addition to the bathroom with its tiny tin shower, the room came with a kitchenette where I made a peanut butter and jelly sandwich every morning to eat at work. Each morning the cockroaches and I fought a duel. The kitchen sink was crawling with them when I woke up, and I would let water run for a few minutes to wash them down the drain. I won every time. Dad would be proud.

I didn't only drive tractors, sometimes I fed the animals or pickaxed dried shit off the floor of the pigsty. The latter was hard work but not smelly because the shit had the consistency of brick. The worst job was helping Herman castrate a pig. When he asked me to help I had no idea what I was in for.

"Hold his legs," Herman told me. "No, you have to hold tighter than that."

The young hog fought with surprising strength as I pinned his legs down, but that was as nothing to how hard he fought in a minute. To my horror, Herman opened his pocketknife and deftly sliced the pig's scrotum open. Somehow I had expected a more surgical procedure, sterilized instruments, maybe local anesthesia. Do not let anyone tell you that animals don't feel pain every bit as much as we do, or that they have less will to live. The pig's squealing was surprisingly human, a soul-searing shriek of pain and terror, and I could only think of a human baby.

I wanted to let go and tell Herman "I quit," but I couldn't. I worked for him and he had asked me to do this. But I vowed—as I pinned the pig's legs to the ground—never to do this again. If Herman asked, I'd refuse. To my relief, he never asked again.

The amount of life in a field was unbelievable to this suburban-slicker. Ground animals, birds, crops growing taller by the minute. I once saw something glisten at the base of a row of corn and stopped the tractor to take a look. Eight tiny, semi-translucent eggs. Their mother had tried to hide them from the hawks that circled overhead. I wondered what they were. They were the size of bird eggs, but with a gelatinous shell. I wanted to break one open and see what kind of animal was inside. Did I have the right? No, not really, but I broke one anyway, reasoning that nature assumed some eggs wouldn't survive until hatching, which is why there were so many. Inside the shell was a baby snake, curled up like an inchworm. It uncurled while I watched, and I felt horrible for what I had done. To make amends, I gathered the remaining eggs in my hands and carried them to a line of trees at the edge of the field. I deposited the eggs in the most protected niche I could find and hoped for the best. In the broader scheme of life, humans are bit players.

Midwestern thunderstorms roar across the prairie with such speed and power that they should have another name to differentiate them from eastern thunderstorms. I was driving my tractor in a corn field far from the farmhouse one afternoon when I saw a storm cloud forming on the western horizon. Given that the land was almost flat I had an unimpeded view. Every time I turned at the eastern end of a row and faced the storm, it seemed to have doubled in size and grown ominously darker. The top of the storm cloud was anvil-shaped.

After twenty minutes in which the storm didn't appear to get closer, I turned at the end of a row and realized the storm was racing toward me. It had made up the distance in a single bound. The storm cloud had ruler-straight edges and the density and mass of dirty concrete. I simply couldn't believe how fast it was approaching or how huge it was. If lightning struck, I was a sitting duck.

I gunned the tractor and headed towards the safety of the farmhouse but feared I couldn't outrun the storm. A tractor moves with all deliberate speed, takes its time under the best of circumstance. Lightning on the way? Your problem, buddy, not mine.

I was seriously scared. I kept glancing over my shoulder. By now the storm had reached the end of the field, its leading edge a blade, its anvil top towering into the sky.

When the storm was upon me I saw that the leading edge was a curtain of solid rain, as true as a carpenter's plumb line. All at once the rain punched me; no warning drops, just a deluge. One second dry air, the next under a waterfall. It was almost worth the risk of getting struck by lightning to experience something this powerful.

Somehow I escaped death, but the sky that evening had a melancholy glow. The men in their rockers seemed mellow. Beginnings and endings, the sky signaled. As darkness grew, the talk turned to the old days.

"You remember Homer Jenkins's place?" Carl asked down the row of rocking chairs.

"Out on Little Hollow Road?" the Greek chorus answered.

"That's him. Tried to raise fifty head of cattle on that tiny piece of land, damn fool."

"Dumb as a nigger."

"Right you are, Fred." Carl chuckled, a chuckle that echoed down the row of rocking chairs. I was horrified, not just by the words but by the nonchalance of the racism. Everyday racism, no less horrifying for being casual.

I stood up. "Think I'll call it a night," I said.

"Thunderstorm tire you out?"

I tried to smile. "Something like that."

"See you tomorrow."

I didn't join the men on the porch the next night, or the next, or the night after that.

—⁓—

During the course of the summer, I had become reasonably adept at fixing my tractor's minor problems but sometimes had to ask Herman for help. A few days after I stopped sitting on the porch, the plow I was pulling kept breaking loose. Fortunately I was in a field near the farmhouse. I found Herman in the barn.

"The plow keeps unhitching. I tried to fix it but couldn't."

Herman just grunted. He hoarded words the way a man in a desert hordes the last drops of water in his canteen.

Herman got his toolbox, and we walked to where the tractor and plow were standing idle. He kneeled down to work with no words, only the occasional grunt.

After a frustrating few minutes, he stood, and I could tell how agitated he was. Herman was normally a kind man, not openly friendly but gentle in spirit. "Goddammit, goddammit all to hell."

He took a pipe wrench from his toolbox and asked me to help him unstick a bolt which had seized up. Even with the two of us tugging on the long handle as hard as we could, the bolt wouldn't budge.

To my surprise—would I ever know enough not to be surprised by people?— Herman rose to his feet and started banging the tractor with the wrench, setting off a terrible clanging. He swung with all his might, swearing without cease. Clang, clang. Fuckin' goddamn sonofabitch. Clang, clang, clang. Motherfucking piece of shit.

He hit the tractor with such force he left big dents in the metal. He kept swinging and swearing, until it almost sounded like music. Clang, clang, clang. Motherfucking goddamn sonofabitching piece of shit. Clang, clang, clang. Finally he calmed down and became as docile as a washed and powdered baby.

"I'll have to get the John Deere people out here. You can work in the barn in the meantime."

"Will do," I said, timidly.

After a week or two of avoiding the men on the porch, twilight loneliness drove me to sit down. No one said anything at first. Then Carl, "You been avoiding us?"

I rocked. "Nothing like that."

"Wouldn't blame you if you were. I'd avoid us if I could. We missed you." Murmurs of ascent down the row. "Got a legal question I want to ask."

"Remember, I'm just a law student."

"You know more than me. Say I want to sue Fred for telling bad jokes. How do I go about it?"

Fred was the guy in the middle of the row whose casual racism had driven me from the porch. He smiled, delighted to be the center of attention.

I was conflicted. These guys might be racists, but I had known them for weeks and knew they were fundamentally good people, kind to each other, quick to help anyone in need. Until now, I hadn't realized one could be simultaneously a racist and a good person.

"I would go to the county courthouse and file a suit of replevin."

"What's replevin?"

"When you want to get something of yours back. Fred stole your sense of humor and you want it back."

"But Fred has no sense of humor."

"That's my point."

Fred slapped his knee in delight. Guffaws down the row. Carl looked nonplused for a second, then joined in the laughter.

—◊—

Herman and Mrs. Knipp invited me to their house for lunch several times that summer. The living room and dining room were dark and full of furniture. Shelter was the purpose of the house. Lunch was the biggest meal of their day. It reminded me of a minor-key Thanksgiving dinner at my grandmother's house. Mrs. Knipp was a shy woman with sun-baked skin, who kept urging me to eat. Herman ate with purpose, not saying much until he finished. Running a farm requires knowledge of soil conditions, plant and animal husbandry, market prices, and weather, but it also requires management skills of a high order. If I had learned anything about Herman, it was that he took his work seriously. Devoting brain cells to small talk was a waste of time.

I learned from Mrs. Knipp that she wasn't the only Knipp who had heart problems, Herman did too. Would Mrs. Knipp wind up living all alone on the farm? Would Herman end up sitting on the hotel porch? When they spoke of their son it was with pride that he had the courage to strike out on his own, and sadness that he was gone. I assumed he'd come back if one of his parents needed him.

I stopped by the house to say goodbye on the day I left. "Herman's not here. He didn't expect you so soon," Mrs. Knipp said.

"I know, I wanted to get an early start."

"He went up to Boonville to get supplies. Should be back by noon. Can you wait?"

"I'm afraid not. I want to get as far as I can today. Classes start day after tomorrow. Say goodbye for me."

"He'll be so sorry to miss you. He says you did a good job."

I had made considerable progress in my thinking during the summer. I reached no conclusions on how to live my life, but had begun to come to grips with my personality and confronted most of my fears.

Most but not all. On my last day working the fields, I leaned against a tree at noon to eat my peanut butter and jelly sandwich. Nothing dented the horizon except the windbreak. Having little competition, the tree I was sitting under seemed unusually tall. I had conquered my fear of heights long enough to attach my radio antenna to our backyard tree—could I climb a tree in the middle of nowhere for no reason other than to prove I could?

Only one way to find out. I brushed the bread crumbs off my hands. The top of the tree seemed to disappear into the sky, a Jack and the Beanstalk tree. I had to jump to reach its lowest branch.

I reconnoitered on the lowest branch then began to climb. Self-consciousness and adrenaline countered my fears until I stopped half-way up to catch my breath. Big mistake. In the future when I climbed a tree for no reason, I'd keep moving. Life Lesson number...? I had lost count of the summer's life lessons. The ground below looked unforgiving, and the bark felt rough. I didn't belong here. But I kept climbing. The ground receded faster than I climbed.

I panicked near the top. Determination had kept me climbing but now the pit of my stomach told me that if I fell from this height, I wouldn't escape with a broken leg, I was done for. This was a dumb, dumb idea.

I scrambled to the top and took one quick glance around. The horizon seemed farther away, the field bigger, the sky wider. Everything seemed bigger except me.

I started down. When I jumped from the lowest branch onto the ground, I felt an overwhelming sense of "Welcome Home."

CHAPTER THIRTEEN

Europe

I HAD ENTERED law school the year the nation's social fabric began to tear. In the five years between John Kennedy's assassination and Robert Kennedy's assassination, every assumption about what kind of country America was and what kind it should be was upended. Martin Luther King was assassinated, cities erupted, and racial peace seemed more elusive than ever. Lyndon Johnson chose to escalate the Vietnam War, while hippies chanted "make love, not war" and preached cooperation over competition. Were we a peace loving nation or a militaristic nation bent on war? Was individual competition the best motivator or could more be accomplished through cooperation? And then there was sex—a gift from God or the work of the Devil? Did we have common values any longer?

Everyone was affected, even people who had cut themselves off from the human race. In my third-floor room, I felt more isolated than I had on the Midwestern prairie. I did little but study. At the beginning of the year I adopted a cat to keep me company. Before the end of the school year, the cat ran away.

I had glimpsed over the summer what life could be like out of my shell. There was far more to it than I had been aware of. When I compared my two farm summers, I realized that I had been too depressed the first time to appreciate what I was seeing but during the second was able to glimpse the munificence of life. The glimpses sustained me for a few months of my second year at law school, but by the middle of the year, I was depressed again. I worried that I had buried myself too deeply, that I could only surface in the safety of the natural world, that in the human world I was a misfit.

There were times I was unable to reply to my roommate's simple questions because I felt so deeply buried. If I could give advice to a prospective law school student, it would be that law school is not a good place to work out your emotional problems.

My fellow second-year students were zeroing in on their careers. I was giving thought to practicing law for a year to see if I liked it better than law school. Other than that I had no clear direction.

As I headed into the summer between second and third year with no clear career plans, I wondered what Dad would think if he knew what I had gone through since graduating from college. As usual, I hadn't told him. The only time I confided in Dad was when I was thinking of applying to law school, and had sought his advice in a pro forma way. He replied to my question something along the lines of, it doesn't matter what career you choose as long as you get on the ladder.

I had worked in Washington, San Francisco, Chicago, Missouri, and on a boat to Europe, but all I had seen of other countries was the inside of a German hospital room. In this, my final summer as a student, I traveled through Western Europe, staying in youth hostels and cheap hotels. I left for Europe the day after final exams ended, and returned to Cambridge the day before classes began in September.

Europe was a revelation. I couldn't believe that a whole continent of people lived more or less the way I wanted to. There was an attention to daily life that was missing in the States. Bread, for example. In the States, Wonder Bread was the standard. Seems impossible now. It was true then. Even a non-foodie like me had known something was lacking, something that turned out to be commonplace in Europe. Good, honest bread. Many varieties of it. People stopped by their local bakery every evening to buy freshly baked bread for dinner. An attention to daily life. Even in major cities like Rome and Paris, life was lived on a personal scale.

And European cities predated cars, which meant they were designed to be walkable. This grounded the cities, gave them human scale. And if you didn't want to walk, there was much better public transportation than in the States.

I traveled at first with a law school classmate I barely knew. As we got to know each other, we realized we had nothing in common and didn't want to see the same places (pre-planning was lacking), so we amicably split up, and I joined a group of three young men from New York I met at Tivoli Gardens in Copenhagen. We traveled from country to country in a rented car, rarely staying in one place for more than a few days. We saw England, France, Germany, Italy, and Spain. We saw Denmark, Norway, Sweden, and the Low Countries. We saw Austria, Switzerland, and tiny Liechtenstein. Every Western European country except Finland and Greece.

For good measure, we crossed the Berlin Wall at Checkpoint Charlie and saw East Berlin. Each country was different but all were built on a human scale—except for East Berlin with its massive Soviet style flats. I loved Norway and Paris the best.

Europe also inspired my creative side, which I hadn't known I had. In Bergen, Norway, I found a paperback copy of *The Grapes of Wrath* which I devoured, and in art museums like the Louvre and the Uffizi, I began a lifelong love affair with art. It pleased me to find that streets in Europe were named after artists and writers, not just statesmen. For every public place that showcased a monumental statue of a general on a rearing horse, there was another with a statue of Balzac. For every rue Bonaparte, there was a rue Voltaire or an Avenue Victor Hugo.

I came back from Europe having found a continent and a way of life that felt right for me.

Having found a place, and having made a decision to quit law after one year of practice, I relaxed a little. I decided to take my head out of the law and spend part of my time working with humans. Through the Harvard volunteer office I took a part-time position at a settlement house in the South End running an afterschool program for grade school boys. It reminded me of the day camp on the Near North Side of Chicago where

I had worked, except that the program was held indoors and the kids did not come from Appalachia. Every afternoon I took the subway across the Longfellow Bridge to Boston where I planned programs, played games, and provided a role model for kids who, for the most part, came from broken families.

—❊—

I made a second decision that year. To write. I had no reason to think I could except for my English professor's encouragement ("finding a student who can write as well as you is what an English teacher lives for") and my instinct upon reading Steinbeck (after *The Grapes of Wrath* I read *The Log from the Sea of Cortez*, and *Travels with Charley*) hadn't worn off.

When I read Steinbeck, I understood everything he did, how he did it, and felt I could do it too. Not that I could write as well as Steinbeck, but that I had it in me to write. I contrasted that with how I felt when I was playing at the Crosstown and contemplating a musical career, and realized I could never be great. I didn't have the instinctive knowledge of musical structure that the true pros have (I learned that from playing alongside true pros for six months).

I didn't feel the same limitations about writing. I felt in my bones how sentences are formed and combined. I knew how to do it even before I did it. I was self-aware enough to know I might be fooling myself, but confident enough to try.

With that realization, the pieces of my life over the past six or seven years fell into place. My drive to understand how other people live, to see as many parts of the world as possible, to try as many occupations as I could, were, I could see now, fodder for my writing. I had been moving toward a purpose without knowing it. A huge life lesson—pay heed to the thinking part of your brain but trust your instincts.

On the other hand (law school had not been wasted on me), writing was so far removed from anything in my family background, so far removed from the world I had grown up in, that I assumed I was partly if not entirely nuts to try. Confident I could do it, and nuts to try.

Those two things, social work and writing, made third year the best year of law school for me. I felt liberated. I dated (I hadn't the first two dismal years), I went to parties, I had a good time.

My grades that year were the best of my law school career.

Graduation from Harvard Law School, 1966
(left to right) *Bill Rogers, Doug, Tony, Jeff*

CHAPTER FOURTEEN

The Law

I JOINED BROWN, Wood, Fuller, Caldwell & Ivey, a midsize Wall Street law firm whose clients included Merrill Lynch, Hoover vacuum cleaners, and the manufacturer of Checker Cabs. I lived on West Houston Street in the Village and took the subway to work. When I was feeling energetic, I walked. My roommate was a classmate from law school.

As a junior associate, I spent most of my time in the firm's law library researching cases for the partners. One question I researched was, does New York law permit the installation of plexiglass security shields in taxis? My research convinced me it did and I so told the partner who had assigned me the case. New Yorkers, listen up. If you like the plexiglass shields, you have me to thank; if you don't like them, blame my partner.

I hated New York. The air was so filthy that when I blew my nose in the morning, the snot came out black. Cars parked on the street overnight had soot-covered windshields in the morning (the squeegee guys who lay in wait at stoplights served a semi-useful purpose). The screeching of the subway drove me nuts. Some people thrive on chaos, I loathe it.

My father had returned to private practice after leaving the government. Because my father split his time between his Washington and New York offices, he and my mother had purchased an apartment in the U.N. Plaza on the East River. Robert Kennedy, who had succeeded my father as attorney general, lived in the building too, and once when I was waiting for the elevator after visiting my parents, the doors opened and there was Kennedy, staring me down as if daring me to enter. He had an aide with him but other than the two of them the elevator was empty. He was not a physically imposing man, but his stare was so intimidating I waited for the next elevator.

I didn't see my parents often, but when I did, my father seemed content with my career. Our arguments were more likely to be about politics than me. I had supported Nixon in 1960 but since had become a Democrat. Dad was a liberal Republican (remember them?), so we weren't light years apart politically, but he so loved to argue that he'd take the opposite side of almost any question for a chance to win. I still felt stiff when I was with him, but compared to the years I lived at home, it was a breeze.

When he was relaxed and not competing, he could be the wittiest, most charming of men. He never put on airs. He didn't lack for ego or vanity, but he never considered himself important. He used to say, "Take your job seriously, don't take yourself seriously," and he lived by that rule. When he went to the restaurants he and Mother favored, he loved it when the maître d' made a fuss about him, but he treated the waitstaff with respect. I have been with important men who take delight in humiliating people below their rank. Not Dad. I like to think that he remembered his improbable journey from the far northern reaches of New York State to the power centers of the nation.

The practice of law did not make me happy. Granted, there were many other kinds of law I could've picked for my one year of practice, but I wanted it to be a kind of law that I was unlikely to return to, if by some chance I changed my mind and wanted to practice law in the future. My other reason was to save enough money to live in Europe until I could find a job there.

Starting salaries at Wall Street law firms were tiny compared to today ($8,000 then, $160,000 plus bonuses now). To earn more money, I moonlighted during tax season at a storefront tax preparer in the Bronx. The neighborhood was poor and most of the tax returns I filled out were simple, but I was not an expert and was terrified I was going to mess up the refund of someone who could ill afford to lose a penny. I remember riding the elevated back to Manhattan many a night with my fingers crossed.

Security is a powerful drug, and more than once its lure made me reconsider my plan to leave law after a year. To give up what was a sure thing to move to Europe and write seemed ludicrous. Not to mention squandering the money my parents had spent to put me through law school. My future would be set if I stayed, a house in Westchester County, membership in a country club. My father had pushed hard for me to take up golf. Golf was a bonding experience, he said, a way to meet and get to know men who could help me in my career. I had taken a few lessons once upon a time and actually gotten a hole-in-one my first year at summer camp (I was nine; it was a very short hole), but golf bored me. And I couldn't see myself living in the suburbs. Still, being able to know what my future would look like and know I'd be financially secure was very seductive.

The closer I got to telling the firm I was leaving, the stronger the pull to stay. Pushing back against it was the memory of the years I had spent trying to find myself without turning my back on Dad. You only have one more step to take, why stop now? Europe was a place I could be myself; a life in the law was not.

As a measure of how locked in I was, I was more worried about telling the firm than telling my father. Wrong, wrong, wrong.

It was the spring of 1967. I had been with my law firm for a year. Because I was not in the habit of confiding in my parents, they had no inkling I was thinking of leaving. They must have guessed something was up when I invited myself over for dinner, but if so, they didn't let on.

The view from their living room was spectacular. My mother loved to watch the river at night when it was too dark to see the boats, when all you could see were their lights. In contrast to the dazzling brightness of Manhattan, the moving pinpoints of light on the dark East River had a special poignancy. The dining room was next to the living room, separated by a little kitchen. As usual, Mother did the cooking. She never wanted a maid in either home because she knew what Dad liked to eat, and because she just wasn't that kind of person. Ironically, her mother— my grandmother—had a year-round live-in maid who would prepare Thanksgiving dinners for us, except for the cranberry sauce which my grandmother refused to let anyone but herself make.

Dad liked two drinks before dinner. He preferred Scotch for many years, then switched to martinis. One could calibrate his career by the evolution of his drinks, his Scotch years ending with single malts, his martini years with Tanqueray gin. I never saw him have more than two of either. I remember his ritual of mixing the gin and vermouth in a glass pitcher and stirring it with a glass rod.

"How's Jeff doing?" I asked after we sat down in the dining room. Jeff was in his first year at Harvard Medical School after graduating from Dartmouth.

Mother beamed. "Great, just great. And Doug loves Cornell." My mother was active in Cornell alumni activities as was my sister. Jeff and I were the black sheep in the family, not having gone to Cornell.

"How's work going?" Dad asked.

"That's what I wanted to talk to you about. Let's wait until we finish dinner."

Mother looked askance. "Is something wrong, dear?"

"No, Mother. I'll explain later. Don't worry, work's going fine. My performance review was excellent." A slight exaggeration, but not an egregious one.

"A man of mystery, huh?" Dad was in a good mood.

"You know me."

He laughed sotto voce. "Not well, actually."

I smiled back. "Same here."

"Let me guess. You're engaged," Dad said.

"Nope. Try again."

"You've been indicted."

I laughed. I was covering up my nervousness well. Indeed, I was enjoying this. Why didn't we have lighthearted conversations like this more often?

"You got a girl pregnant."

"Yikes, no."

"Adele, take a guess," Dad said to my mother.

"I have no idea, dear."

"Take a guess."

"Really, I have no idea."

"You have to take a guess. Come on."

My mother shrugged. "He bought … a new suit."

I laughed. "Mother?"

"Adele, you're not taking this seriously," Dad said.

"I have no idea, dear." A touch of exasperation, very rare for Mother.

"You'll both find out soon enough," I said. Mother looked relieved. It was telling of Mother that even her expressions of relief passed through a filter of good manners.

I helped Mother clean up and then we joined Dad in the living room. The curtains were open inviting the non-magical lights of Long Island, and the magical lights of the invisible boats, into the wide room.

Dad looked comfortable on the sofa. Mother joined him, and I sat in the arm chair. "I've decided to leave the law."

"The firm?" Dad seemed confused

"No, the law."

"Tony, what are you talking about?"

"I'm going to give my notice tomorrow."

"And then what?"

"I've got a plane ticket to Paris. I'm leaving Saturday. I'm going to write." I was focusing on Dad's face, but I glimpsed a stricken look on Mother's. In the millisecond it registered, I read it as expressing fear of what Dad's reaction would be more than horror at what I was saying. Why was she so worried? I assumed he'd be concerned and worried at first, but in my naivete also assumed he'd be happy I had found my way.

Dad stood. For a moment he sputtered. Then, "Tony, this is the most reckless thing you've ever done. You must be out of your mind. What makes you think you can write? Have you ever written anything?" He calmed a little. He was a capable man who had accomplished much, and you don't get to be as accomplished as he by being a hothead. "I can understand why you want to write. If I hadn't gone into law, I'd probably be a journalist. But throwing away a law degree to write? I've never heard of such a foolish thing. Why can't you stay at your firm and write at night?"

I stood and went to the window. Looking out I said, "I have written a few things this year to see if I can. I can't write and practice law at the same time, the law's too demanding. If I want to see how good a writer I am, I have to throw myself into it. I've always wanted to live in Europe and this will give me a chance to do that too."

"Always?"

"Okay, since last summer. Damn it, Dad, I thought you'd understand." I never swore with or at my parents. There was no swearing in our house in Bethesda, and I hadn't picked up the habit.

"Oh, I understand all right. I understand that you're spoiled rotten. You expect hosannas without having to lift a finger."

"What are you talking about? I have a J.D. from Harvard Law School. You think that was easy?"

"Which you are throwing away. Do you know how many young men out there would kill for a Harvard Law degree?"

"Are you projecting your feelings on me?"

Dad fumed. "Stop psychoanalyzing me. That's your way of ducking. Face yourself squarely. You're running away. Life is too much for you. You've never had what it takes to make it in the real world."

Twenty years of pent-up resentment exploded in a string of words I had never uttered before in my life, let alone directed at my father. "Fuckin' asshole," was the mildest form of endearment. I swore like Herman Knipp swore at tractors. Lucky thing I didn't have a pipe wrench. "How can you not understand? Haven't you even glimpsed what I've been going through?"

"What are you talking about?"

"You haven't noticed me struggling to distance myself from you without turning my back on you?"

"As opposed to getting ahead, like you should have been?"

I couldn't stand looking at his face anymore. I turned away. "You are so fucking practical. Have you never had a dream? Not once, in your insecure, driven, overly competitive life?"

Quietly, "I dreamed of getting out of Norfolk. I dreamed of using the talent I had to build a better life for myself and my family. I dreamed I could make my dead mother proud."

Normally I'd be touched by his words, I understood the gaping hole his mother's death had left in his young life, but this was one of his standard ploys. When put on the defensive and fury doesn't work, invoke pity.

Mother was purple, not from rage but from worry. Here was a man she stoutly defended against all enemies and her first son duking it out with unprecedented ferocity, and she was helpless to intervene. For a split second I felt sorry for her, but I was on a mission to get everything out in the open, and I wasn't going to stop now.

"Dad, I have to live my life, I can't live yours. You grew up in a different era. Your world must've seemed a much scarier place than mine. Maybe I'd be just like you if I had been born when you were, but I wasn't. Even if I fuck up, even if I fail horribly, I've got to find my own way. To be honest, I think you've been afraid to fail your whole life. I don't blame you, but I don't want to live in fear. My goal is to get as much out of life as I can, not to get as far ahead as I can."

Dad's turn to explode. "You think I was driven by fear? Is that what you think? How dare you? Aren't you grateful for what your mother and I have given you? Do you take that for granted?"

"What's that got to do with it? Of course, I'm grateful."

"So you prove it by saying I'm a fucking asshole driven by fear, and quitting your job?"

"I'm sorry for the swearing, I'll be embarrassed after the smoke blows away, but yes, I think you're insecure and have been all your life, and quitting the law has nothing to do with you. You shouldn't take it personally."

"Really? Quitting the profession that I love? Nothing to do with me, who you've resented your whole life? No slap in the face intended, is that what you're saying?"

"Yes, that's what I'm saying. I haven't thought of it from that angle, to be honest. I guess I should have."

"I'm surprised to hear Mr. Psychoanalysis admit that."

"But I haven't resented you my whole life, that's not the truth. It's much more complicated than that. I'm not leaving the law to hurt you."

"You'd be convicted by a jury of your peers."

"And you'd probably be the prosecutor in the case," I snapped.

On that note the evening ended. There was some more feinting, more stricken looks on my mother's face, but Dad and I were outraged out.

I mumbled thanks for dinner to Mother as I left. I wasn't being sarcastic, but it sounded as if I were.

Dad approached as I was at the door. "When did you say you are leaving?"

"Saturday."

Dad nodded and turned away. I noticed he had a fresh drink in his hand.

He called me the next night. I was startled to hear his voice. "Tony, I had made you the executor of my will. Do you want to remain my executor?"

He sounded near tears. My heart broke. "Of course, Dad."

"Take care," he said. And that was the last time we spoke for a year.

CHAPTER FIFTEEN

Paris

MY LAW FIRM took the news in stride. "You've done good work. Anytime you want your job back, it'll be waiting for you," the senior partner said when I told him I was leaving. I was surprised to hear that. I didn't believe I had done very well. Too preoccupied, lacking in enthusiasm, I thought; the old story.

I wasn't sorry to escape the law library or leave New York, but as I took off I wondered what I was getting into. I had no job, no place to stay, and knew no one in Paris. A few weeks of French lessons were my only preparation. I had saved $1,000 out of my salary and my moonlighting earnings and estimated I could last for six months without a job if I lived frugally, although I hoped to find work much sooner.

It takes distance to see patterns. The checkerboard that is the Midwest is not visible from the ground. It was only when I was in the air on my way to Paris that I realized I was duplicating the jumping-off-a-cliff aspect of my Midwestern summer. Why did I feel the need to go to unfamiliar places without a job or contacts? It wasn't that I was a bold person. If anything, I was overly cautious. A death wish? A test wish?

I decided as I gazed out the window that I was doing what I wanted to do. The testing aspect was an ancillary benefit. The Midwest had beckoned because it was the Heartland. Europe beckoned because I fell in love with it two summers before. As I stepped off the plane in Paris, I was reminded how the Rhythm Rockers felt when we stood on the dock at Bremerhaven. We turned to each other and asked, "What now?"

—᙮᙮—

"What now?" I asked myself. Even with only one suitcase I had a hard time squeezing into the subway to the city. My copy of *Europe On 5 Dollars A Day* gave me the name of several cheap hotels clustered in the student quarter, and that's where I headed.

First thing I noticed when I stood on the sidewalk outside the Maubert Mutualité metro was the ozone in the air. The air didn't smell clogged like New York. It didn't smell clean but it felt stirred (with a glass rod?). I hadn't noticed the difference on my brief stay in Paris during my summer tour of Europe. But standing on the sidewalk knowing I'd be staying, I did.

I could tell that if I stood there too long I'd panic so I climbed the hill to my right. One of the cheap hotels was supposedly on it. I blanched when I came to the hotel. I had low expectations, but this? It made the fleabag in Tipton look respectable. I didn't dare step in, let alone sleep there. I located hotel number two in the warren of streets and decided it was bearable. Climbing three flights behind a rotund hotelier who lacked joie de vivre, I welcomed myself to Paris.

The room had a gabled window, as had my teenage bedroom, but this one looked out on a wedge of tin rooftops and an interior courtyard, not at a ham radio antenna attached (heroically) to a backyard tree. When I opened the window, I heard buses and high heels and voices speaking rapid French. I sat on the bed, which supported me in name only, debating whether to sleep or eat, deciding after due deliberation to eat.

I used the toilet in the hallway, then descended three flights to the street. Again, street sounds, like wind. Silence within the noise. The ozone effect. A cafeteria on the corner.

No need for French. The dishes were laid out on the counter for all to choose. I chose a croissant and boiled egg and coffee, and sat down at a window table. My loneliness wasn't nearly as profound as it had been when I arrived in Tipton. I remembered going downstairs after I checked into the Tipton Hotel and feeling my heart sink into my shoes. That was before I met the old timers. I wondered if there was a Paris equivalent to the Tipton Hotel porch.

I slept for three hours and woke up groggy. For a moment I couldn't remember where I was, then through the open window, I heard the distinctive street sounds and knew I was in Paris.

In the afternoon I walked and walked and walked. To the river, along the river to St Germain des Pres, across the river to the Louvre, to the Champs Élysées and back again to the Left Bank. I ate at the same cafeteria, returned to my room, and slept the sleep of the jet-lagged and happy.

To be in a place you plan to stay is different than passing through. During my first days there my eye didn't seek out the high points like a tourist, it took everything in. Sure, I visited Notre Dame and the Eiffel Tower, sure I sat at sidewalk cafés and sipped the occasional coffee (being parsimonious in the extreme), but mostly I just walked, feet on autopilot, mind wide open.

Paris had not yet undergone its mandated cleaning, and the buildings for the most part were black with soot. Individually beautiful in form, their facades were breathtaking in combination. If form follows function, and beauty follows form, does beauty follow function? Law school syllogizing notwithstanding, I didn't think so. Beauty is sui generis.

I didn't catch on to the quality of beauty at first. I saw it, but it seemed like tinsel or wrapping paper, something superficial that could be peeled off and discarded. One day, I left the café after my morning coffee just at the moment the sun channeled the length of the boulevard and I saw the curve in the road ahead as a thing of beauty. From then on, even in rain or gloom, the curve looked beautiful to me. The curve made it so, the light made me see.

If I expected my money to last six months, I had to be careful with it, but I hoped to find a job before then. I had no idea how to go about finding a job. With very little French and no working papers, my options were limited. Indeed, now that I was facing the reality of Paris,

Rue des Ursins, Paris

my prospects seemed nonexistent. *What Was I Thinking?* would be the name of my first book, a thick, encyclopedic compilation of stupid assumptions and bad decisions.

For several weeks, I relished being alone in a foreign city. Living abroad was not commonplace then, and I felt as if I had flipped dimensions, which was exactly the effect I hoped to achieve. To see where you have come from, you have to leave. Eventually, loneliness reached me, and I sought company. I had resolved not to seek out Americans, but gave in to necessity.

The American Center for Students and Artists was on Boulevard Raspail. An imposing stone building of no charm, the Center hosted events and served as a meeting place where Americans could meet the French, and vice versa. Most of the Americans were students. One of them, a young man named Terry, became my friend. Terry was taking graduate courses at the Sorbonne. Through Terry, I met a young Frenchwoman whose family lived in a venerable old apartment building in the prosperous 16th arrondissement, and through the young woman, I rented a room on the seventh floor. Looked at from the outside, the seventh floor had a charming tin roof; from inside, the seventh floor consisted of tiny rooms with no heat where the servants of the wealthy residents used to live. On one side of me lived a Portugese laborer, on the other an American student. My window was in the curved tin roof, and when I lay in bed, I was looking at the sky.

There was no elevator to the seventh floor, so I quickly learned to ration my trips outdoors, and there was no bath or shower, only a cold water spigot in the hallway next to the toilet which served everyone on the floor. To shave, I bought a hot plate to heat spigot water, and a plastic basin to carry the waste water back to the spigot. My rent was $17 per month.

To make my money last, I ate bread and jam in my room and heated water for my breakfast coffee. To reduce trips up and down the stairs, I brought the bread the night before. I tried many different types of bread before I found one that didn't go stale overnight. There was a tiny table in the room, and after I finished my breakfast, I began to write. Badly. Why didn't sentences fall into place on paper the way they did in my mind? The stories I had written while practicing law were better than this. Yuck.

I needed a job. Through the American Center, I found part-time work at a boys school in Neuilly-sur-Seine, a well-to-do suburb just west of Paris. The school was run by nuns, and I was hired to keep order in the lunchroom and teach sports to the boys at recess. Tony. Sports. Dad, are you listening?

The job paid $75 a month. With careful budgeting (breakfast in my room, lunch at the school, $1.25 steak frites for dinner, and one beer per week), I figured I could get by on $100 per month, covering the gap between expenditures and pay with money saved from my law practice and my tax moonlighting.

I worked from late morning until mid-afternoon, commuting to work via bus. There is nothing that brings the romance of Paris down-to-earth like a daily bus commute. In a relatively few weeks, I was living in Paris in mind and spirit as well as body. The switch to a parallel dimension was complete. And what I realized was that I liked Paris even stripped of its illusions. Living here would not have to become an entry in my ledger, *What Was I Thinking?*

I had moved here with no time limit in mind. As far as I was concerned, I had moved here for good. What came after this job was something I hadn't considered. I was off to a good start, and that was all I cared about.

CHAPTER SIXTEEN

Paris II

To MOVE TO A NEW country is to become a child again. Everything needs to be relearned: language, customs, the unwritten rules, of which France has plenty. Don't smile unless you mean it. Don't say bonjour without appending monsieur or madame. Don't assume that sitting elbow to elbow with a person in a café or bistro gives you license to talk to them.

English was not common in Paris in the late sixties, and one's French pronunciation was expected to be perfect. Maddening, but it was their country. I hated to hear Americans raise their voices when their English wasn't understood. One Sunday as I was drinking my beer of the week at a café, I overheard a young American man complaining to the waiter, "There's no lettuce and tomato in my sandwich." When the waiter didn't understand, the young man shouted, "THERE'S NO LETTUCE AND TOMATO IN MY SANDWICH." Which made me want to punch out the jerk.

Of course, it was not unheard of for a French person to feign not knowing English, either out of annoyance at the uncouth or as a ploy to force the foreigner to speak perfect French or else. In that case, a game of language chicken ensued. Who would crack first? As long as you treated it as sport, a kind of jousting, you were fine. Get huffy, and you lose.

That's what competition was like in France. A sport, a game. No one took it seriously. What was taken seriously was theory. Get your theory right. Make it elegant. Many nights after work, I headed over to the American Center and listened to the young French people who hung out there honing their theory-chops. An old joke has one Frenchman saying to another, "Your idea is fine in practice, but does it work in theory?" Never while I lived in Paris did a French person inquire what I did. When I asked a young French woman why not, she replied because the French are less inclined to define themselves by their jobs than Americans. "We work to earn a living, but live to do other things." She mentioned a friend who worked as a bank teller to support his mountain climbing.

Commuting to work on a Parisian bus provided a new platform for thinking. The snug suburbs of my youth had provided my first platform, the Midwestern prairie a very different kind of platform, and Paris yet another. The triangulation theory. To see something clearly you have to see it from at least three angles.

My conclusion while commuting: there is no universal template for how to live, only universal striving. Meaning does not come ready-made or guaranteed. Each person must craft his own. Climbing the ladder is not for all. The view from the top probably is nice, but I preferred to observe life from ground level.

Then write about it. Which still was a problem. If my writing had improved over the first weeks in Paris, I couldn't see it. I remembered the books that had moved me. *A Farewell to Arms*, read in high school, was the first novel in which the characters came alive for me; in college, *Crime and Punishment* showed me how deeply a novel could probe human psychology, and literature from Asia showed me how the western world's outlook on life is not universal, even though the underlying truths of life are. If I could do for others even a fraction of what books like those and *The Grapes of Wrath* had done for me, I'd be thrilled.

The jury was still out on whether I could. In fact it had fled the courthouse in horror at my first scribblings, and the judge in my trial was finding it hard to convene a new jury.

But I still believed I understood the bones, the skeletal structure of fiction. I regretted having rejected my English professor's advice to pursue the study of literature. I had a lot of lost time to make up. Being in France it seemed appropriate to start with Flaubert. *Madame Bovary* hadn't done anything for me in college, but this time Flaubert's prose (in the Steegmuller translation) and the letters Flaubert wrote to his lover Louise Colet as he struggled to write *Bovary*, were inspiring. I read contemporary American novels like *Sometimes A Great Notion*, messy, sprawling novels, meant to convey the expansiveness and freedom of America but from across an ocean seemed claustrophobic and superficial in comparison to *Madame Bovary*. Less is more, indeed.

I settled into my daily rhythm. Buy a thick loaf of bread the night before, eat it in my room with jam and instant coffee the next morning, walk down seven flights to the street, take the bus to work, take the bus home, repeat after me. The kids at the school were fun. Most were English. A few gave me trouble of the well-bred sort, but they were outnumbered by the impeccably mannered.

Unless it was pouring at recess, I'd take them outside to the small playground attached to the school. The playground was cut off from Neuilly by a high slat fence. I found it hilarious that I was teaching the boys soccer which I didn't know how to play. My instruction to the kids about soccer was remember to kick, not throw. At lunchtime my job was to be the token male authority figure in a school run by nuns, the easiest job I ever had, thanks to the order instilled by the nuns and the general good deportment of the boys.

The head nun was a benevolent dictator, Jesus-sweet in manner, tough as nails inside. She could kneecap you or bless you with equal alacrity. One afternoon the head nun introduced me to a visiting nun when I happened to be wearing a black turtleneck and black blazer. The visiting nun said, "Nice to meet you, Father," which sent the head nun into a fit of giggles followed by a frown stern enough to carve permanent grooves in her forehead.

The older nuns had an arms-length relationship to the human race, reserving their affection for Jesus, but the young nuns treated me like a human being. One in particular, Sister Jeanne, befriended me. She was from Liverpool and had spent her childhood in India. She had an avid curiosity and peppered me with questions about the United States. "Why are there so many murders?" "Is it true that anyone can buy a gun?" "Have you ever been to Hollywood?" I would linger after school to chat with her. I found her easy to get along with.

Once I got used to Paris, I did meet women. One advantage of living in Europe is that it's easy to meet people from different countries, in fact, it's unavoidable. An education in and of itself, but nothing lasting resulted until the very end. More often than not, I spent nights alone in my room listening to Radio Caroline on a cheapo radio I had bought when I got to Paris. The songs of the time were "Whiter Shade of Pale" and "All You Need Is Love."

In mid-winter I was forced by the specter of freezing to death to buy a space heater. When I got home from dinner or the American Center, the first thing I'd do is turn on the space heater, then jump into bed fully clothed until the room heated up (relatively speaking). Then I'd slip out of bed long enough to put on pajamas and slide under the covers again. With a bedside lamp to read by and Radio Caroline to listen to, the cold could be quite cozy.

A young woman directly across the street was in the habit of dressing and undressing without closing her curtains. I had to stand by my window to see her because of the slope of my gabled window, but she either didn't notice or didn't mind being watched. At first it was va-va-voom, then it was pull the damn curtains why don't you?

I loved the look of the sky above the tin roofs after it snowed, which it rarely did and never more than an inch or two. Gray, white against bright blue. Paris blue is something else, penetrating without being harsh, softened by the reflected gray of the tin roofs.

The United States did not look good from a distance. The Vietnam war seemed an example of hypocrisy from a nation that thumps its chest over the virtues of democracy then acquiesces when the South Vietnamese government voids election results the U.S. doesn't like. The U.S. poverty rate seemed unconscionable as seen from the vantage point of a country that provided a substantial, effective safety net to its citizens. France had tight gun control laws and no death penalty. France just seemed more civilized. Granted its long history included internal strife, cowardice, and an imperfect record of racial tolerance, but alongside that checkered history, France had evolved a stunning civilization.

Why would I ever want to return to the U.S.?

I didn't give any thought to this question until I had lived in Paris for six months. Until then, my time was spent adjusting to my new life. My goal when I arrived had been to settle down and write. I vaguely assumed I'd live in Europe permanently. Now I began to wonder if staying here was what I wanted. I liked it better than the States, but America had the advantages of home: language, customs, understanding the values and people, ease of life in a country whose habits I knew intimately.

Before I arrived in France I hadn't given any thought to what it would be like to be a foreigner. In the short term it was invigorating, but I came to realize that I would always be a foreigner if I stayed, even if I stayed the rest of my life. Being a foreigner creates a barrier to full understanding of the people and life around you; a porous barrier, to be sure, but a barrier none the less. For someone who wanted to understand as much as he could, that was something to consider.

—ɯ—

I got through the winter in fine spirits. It never got bitterly cold. I had no contact with my father and limited contact with my mother (a few letters). Distances seemed longer then, and I felt completely cut off from America. Which I wanted. I was aware of the distortions of thought that self-imposed exile can bring, but it was healthier than the cave I had dug for myself in my teens and early twenties.

Having established a base in Paris, I felt free to let my mind wander where it may. No expectations to live up to, no one to let down. No fear I'd be caught napping, figuratively speaking. Funny how freely ones thoughts flow when in a compatible country, without expectations other than your own. Descartes would have been proud.

I know I'm alive because I want to stay alive, was the first tenet of my reworking of Descartes. The final piece was an awareness which came to me walking the street below my room one day, that we can never know anything for sure. We make assumptions, have beliefs, and may well be right, but we will never have the distance and objectivity to conclusively prove them. We'd have to live forever and be able to escape our universe to see our short, earthbound lives with any objectivity. Science is the closest thing we have to objectivity, but science is based on measurements and math, and we can't be certain that either apply in other parts of the universe. Wait, you say; the law of nature is the same throughout the universe. But that is only an assumption, and if it is wrong, the house of science would tumble. If our universe is only one of many, as is the current thinking, other universes may have hundreds of dimensions and time may be very different, so how can we be sure our measurements and math are correct in the absolute? And by the way, what is time? Humility must be at the heart of a philosophy if a philosophy is to be true. Humility needs no math or measurement.

This awareness which came to me on a street in Paris certainly wasn't original, several schools of Hellenistic thought cautioned against the hubris of being certain of our knowledge (as of course did Socrates), but it came to me entire, as a fully fleshed out idea, with supporting evidence attached. Proust's madeleine, *The Remembrance of Things Past.* Nice when it happens, which is not often.

CHAPTER SEVENTEEN

Assassinations

ON APRIL 4, Martin Luther King Jr. was assassinated by a lone gunman in Memphis. Cities burned across America. One city was spared, and that was Indianapolis, where Robert Kennedy stood before an angry crowd and spoke as someone who had known violence in his own family. "What we need in the United States is not hatred; what we need in the United States is not violence or lawlessness; but is love and wisdom, and compassion toward one another, and a feeling of justice toward those who still suffer within our country, whether they be white or whether they be black." His aides had urged him to cancel because of danger to his safety, but he went ahead and his words calmed the crowd. For the first time I wished I were back in the States. I hated feeling cut off from such monumental events.

My school took the boys to the French Alps for spring vacation. I went along as a chaperone. We stayed in cabins in the foothills and told ghost stories at night. After the boys were in bed, Sister Jeanne and I had time to talk. I asked her why she had become a nun, and she said because she fell in love with Jesus. I asked if she didn't miss the things other young women were doing, and she said, no, if you know the love of Jesus, you don't need anything else. She wasn't stuffy. She loved it when I teased her about her makeup (she didn't wear any of course) or her choice of clothes. She had a pleasant singing voice and kept the boys entertained by singing songs like "I Am The Walrus." She asked me what I would do when I returned to the States.

"Why do you assume I'm going back?" We were sitting outside the mess tent in the dark. We had the Alps to ourselves.

"The way you talk about the riots. You hate being away, don't you?"

"Until now, I didn't."

"I don't believe you," she said.

I was truly surprised. She was a very understanding soul, not given to challenging what others said.

"Don't be annoyed," she said, seeing my expression, which was no mean feat in the dark.

"I'm surprised you don't believe me."

"You seem like someone who's searching. If you were a different kind of person, I'd spot you as someone who's ripe for Jesus." She shifted her weight on the bench. "But first you need to find out where you belong. Jesus will wait."

"That's nice of him."

"You should feel complimented. I tell most people to find Jesus and everything else will follow. Not you. You'll always be restless if you default to Jesus."

"Very perceptive," I said. The tall Alps loomed above our foothill. Everywhere silence, profound, ancient. "Cheeky but perceptive."

She laughed. "Do you mind?"

"Not coming from you."

"I've been accused of telling others what to do."

I feigned shock. "NO?"

"Oh, stop it." She giggled. She made a fist and pretended to poke my arm, but stopped short of making contact.

It was not long after we returned from the Alps that Paris was consumed by the events of May 1968. A student protest at the Paris University at Nanterre (a working class, very left wing suburb) led to a government shutdown of the university and of the Sorbonne, which led to outrage throughout the student community. Huge protests took place at the Arc de Triomphe and in the Left Bank. The police attacked demonstrators who were trying to get close to the Sorbonne, and the confrontation spread. Barricades were erected, cobblestones ripped from the street to throw at the police, cars set on fire. Hundreds of students and police were injured. Rumors flew of agents provocateurs throwing Molotov cocktails. Workers by the thousands joined the student protestors, and on Monday, May 13, more than one million people marched through the streets of Paris. In sympathy with the protesters, an estimated ten million workers throughout France, two-thirds of the workforce, went out on strike, and Paris all but shut down. The Métro, buses, and trains stopped running. Mail wasn't delivered. Newspapers stopped being distributed. Long distance telephone service was disrupted. Internal flights cancelled. Gas was in short supply, leading to fewer and fewer cars on the street. In a very short space of time, Paris went from being a vibrant, thriving capital to a small provincial town.

I remember the eerie silence when I walked from my building in the mornings. Pedestrians were the only things moving. If you couldn't get where you were going on foot, you didn't get there. My little radio repeatedly reported overnight riots, with hundreds of people wounded, hundreds more arrested. The fear was palpable. My district was largely immune to the violence because few without means lived there, but walking across the river quickly brought me to barricaded streets and burned out cars. Black police vans full of heavily armed men careened through the city. The Paris police were notorious for not being gentle, and I did my best to stay out of their way. Given that I was of student age, I figured I could easily be mistaken for a protester, and since I didn't have working papers, I could be in real trouble if arrested. I ducked my way through the back streets of the Left Bank, avoiding crowds. Burned out cars and impromptu barricades are a shocking sight to see in a civilized city. Civilization is paper-thin, I saw with my own eyes.

I didn't go to work, of course. Few did. Unable to get anywhere, people lived on what they could buy from their corner stores. The clerks at the tabacs became the town criers. A two thousand year old city had been brought to its knees in less than a month.

Headline in British newspaper, Evening Standard

The government of Charles de Gaulle teetered. De Gaulle fled to who knew where (a French military base in Germany to consult with his generals, as it turned out). He reappeared a few days later, dissolved the Parliament, and made a triumphant return to Paris down the Champs Éysées.

The Champs Élysées was not far from my room. I walked there and found a good position on the street. The sidewalks were packed with people, many waving the French tri-colors, some stony-faced and watchful. De Gaulle knew how to do spectacle. Dozens of vehicles escorted the President. In the middle of the entourage, De Gaulle stood in an open car. He had military bearing down to a science, and he was a very tall man to begin with, so he towered over everyone. The sight of him defiant and proud in his open car was commanding. How could he not remain in power?

The protests dissipated quickly after that, and Paris returned to semi-normal. But like the race riots in the States, and all the other turmoil of the sixties, the unrest of May informed everything that came after in France. Race riots in America, Paris all but shutting down. Who could blame those who wanted a return to settled ways? I disagreed with them, but a backlash was inevitable, and schisms opened up in the sixties that have yet to be resolved.

By early June, I was no longer eating breakfast in my room. I hadn't made a firm decision to go home, but I was leaning that way. I hadn't used all the money I had saved from my year of law, and since I'd probably be going home in the not too distant future I could safely spend a little more of it. On June 5, I was eating breakfast at my usual café, having my usual two croissants and a café creme. The waiter knew what I wanted and would get it ready for me as soon as I walked in the door. Nothing in my experience in Paris except maybe riding the bus to work made me feel more like a Parisian.

On my way back to my room, I stopped at a sidewalk kiosk to buy the *Herald Tribune*. The man who ran the kiosk knew by now that I was American, although we never said more to each other than "bonjour." He greeted me with a sad face. "C'est triste, c'est tres triste." I didn't know what he was talking about. What was sad?

His radio was on, and I wondered if he had heard something on the radio that made him sad. I couldn't follow the rapid French coming from the radio. Then came words I understood. *"Robert Kennedy, il est presque mort."*

I ran as fast I as could back to my building and up the seven flights of stairs. Not waiting to catch my breath, I tuned to the BBC on my little shortwave radio. Robert Kennedy had been shot in the head shortly after midnight. He was clinging to life in a Los Angeles hospital, but his condition was grave.

Not this, I thought. Please, not Robert Kennedy. His speeches on the campaign trail had inspired me. JFK, MLK ... now RFK? The country could not take another mortal blow. Please, not this.

I began to weep. I sat on my sagging bed in Paris and felt alone in a way I hadn't before. I wanted to go home.

CHAPTER EIGHTEEN

Odd Jobs

I RETURNED TO THE States in late summer, 1968, married to a Spanish Basque woman I had met two months before I left. She did not speak English and I didn't speak Spanish. It was an impulsive marriage, to say the least, and I am not an impulsive person. My loneliness had reached the breaking point and I thought marriage might cure it. It didn't. The marriage ended in divorce seven years later.

We had two children, David and Veronica, who lived with me and my second wife, Tamara, after we married in 1977. Tamara and I have one son together, Sam. Being a father has meant more to me than anything else in my life.

My first wife and I arrived back in the States at the tail end of Richard Nixon's campaign for president. My father was advising Nixon and occasionally joining him on the campaign trail, but was happy being back in private practice. Lyndon Johnson had done wonderful things for civil rights and Medicare, but was digging us deeper and deeper into Vietnam. My impressionistic imagination believed I could smell lingering smoke from the burning of U.S. cities a few months before. A nasty time. I had the feeling that in the fourteen months I had been away, the hope of the mid-sixties had morphed into sourness and accusation. I regretted not being in the States to understand the changes better, yet the year away had been essential to me. I felt more confident that I could handle my father.

Maybe that's why I chose to live in Arlington, Virginia, across the river from Bethesda, when I could have lived anywhere. Living close to my father felt less threatening now that I had distanced myself by a year away. My plan was to support myself through odd jobs while I continued to write.

In the next two years, I saw my parents more than I had since the summer I lived at home and worked on the sod farm. Weeks would go by when I didn't see them, but they invited my wife and me to dinner, and on occasion I went to sit by the pool and argue Vietnam with my father. Growing up I would have given anything not to have to be near Dad. I was a captive audience then, now I saw him by choice. All the difference in the world.

Certainly I was testing whether my self-confidence was strong enough to have a normal relationship with Dad, but it was more than that. I still hoped to get close to him, and thought there was a better chance now that I had found how I wanted to live.

Neither my father nor I ever mentioned our blowup the night I announced I was quitting law and moving to Paris. It was as if the year of silence hadn't happened. Replacing the silence was an increasingly vigorous argument about Vietnam. To me it was a moral issue—we had stood by while our wholly owned subsidiary, the South Vietnamese government, voided an election which had been won by the communists. Did we support democracy or did we not? Dad and I were like two characters in a play, saying the same lines over and over again. Typical scene in our tranquil dining room with the oil painting of a distant ancestor on the wall—old New England in suburban Maryland.

Dad: Foreign policy is messy. Choices have to be made, some of which may go against our values.

Me: Then what's the point of having values?

Dad: You haven't faced the complexity of the world.

Me: We're sending men over there to die.

Dad knew more about death and war than I, so the last line was a low blow. Dad had served on an aircraft carrier in the Pacific during World War II. His ship, the *Intrepid*, is now a floating museum in New York City. It suffered several kamikaze hits while Dad was on board. I didn't serve in the military. To his credit Dad never compared his wartime service with my lack of service.

When I graduated from law school, I was ordered to report for a physical. The Army had run out of recruits under the age of twenty-six so they were going to start drafting the over twenty-sixes like me. I passed the physical and was told I would be inducted within three weeks. I faced a dilemma. I couldn't claim to be a conscientious objector because I wasn't against all war. I didn't want to flee to Canada and live there the rest of my life; for all my quarrels with America, it was my country. But I believed the Vietnam war was immoral. I decided I would accept induction, but if sent to Vietnam, would refuse to go, which would mean a court martial and probable jail. I didn't know if I'd have the guts to follow through but never had to find out. The three weeks came and went. When months later I dared ask why I hadn't been called, the draft board explained that they had been able to fill their quota from the under twenty-six year olds after all.

Dad had installed a swimming pool in our backyard after he left government. He loved nothing better than to lie in the sun. I hated sunbathing but if I wanted to talk to him, poolside was the best venue.

"You're pale," he said, the first time I saw him after I got back.

"I'm always pale, lest you forget."

"Vitamin D."

"Cancer."

He was lying on his back with his eyes closed, his chest oiled like a model's. "The sun gives me a sense of well-being."

"I can't stand feeling hot."

"How was Paris?"

"I loved it."

"Why did you come back?"

"Still sorting that out. Everything that was going on here made me want to come back."

"Thought it might make you want to run farther away." He could turn words into metal.

"I don't hate my country."

"You criticize it enough."

"We're not looking too good now."

Richard Nixon was the final straw. The prospect of Nixon becoming president appalled me. He was Dad's friend, but I had become convinced that he was paranoid and dishonest. As stubborn as Dad could be, he was neither paranoid nor dishonest, and I couldn't understand why he didn't see what I saw in Nixon. "What's with Nixon's secret plan to end the war? How can anyone fall for that?"

"He wants to gradually wind the war down but doesn't want to tip his hand on the timing."

"So, 'trust me,' is the secret plan?"

"You are pretty cynical about people who are shouldering the burden."

"Subtext, I'm not?"

"Subtext, you have no idea what it's like to run for president."

There was no counter-argument to that. I felt as if I had baked in the sun for hours. I jumped in the pool to cool off. When I emerged dripping wet, Dad had fallen asleep. I wondered if I should wake him so he didn't get sunburned. I decided not to and went inside the house. Mother was in the kitchen, preparing dinner and talking to my wife. "Would you like some iced tea?"

"Sure."

She started toward the refrigerator.

"I'll get it," I said. The kitchen had been remodeled since I lived there. A double-wide refrigerator had been installed. "Dad's fallen asleep outside. Should I wake him?"

"He doesn't burn."

"I burn in under ten minutes."

"You always have. It's good to have you home, dear," she said.

"Good to be home, but Dad and I are going to come to blows over Nixon. Why does Dad stick with him?"

"Your father is a loyal friend."

"Bigger things than friendship are at stake."

"Dick has his flaws but he'll be a good president."

"Would you support him if Dad didn't?"

Mother gave me her look. "I think highly of both Dick and Pat."

"But for president? Really?"

"Tone, I suggest you avoid the subject of Nixon when you're talking to your father." Mother called me Tone in moments of affection or sternness. She was the only person in the world who called me Tone.

"For some reason, I can't."

I went upstairs to take a shower. After I dried off, I got dressed in my former bedroom on the third floor. The room was newly wallpapered with a floral print and was now used as a guest room. The bed had been moved across the room to where my radio station had been. I had saved my shortwave receiver, but given the rest of my equipment away.

I began my odd job period driving a cab (later I delivered phone books, worked on an assembly line in a factory, and sold toys at a department store). To get my "face" (my hack license), I needed to pass a test. Conveniently, prospective drivers were given a cheat sheet listing answers to probable questions, which turned out to be remarkably close to the questions on the test I took. I passed the test.

On my first day I reported to work and was assigned a cab. It was a scary proposition to drive a vehicle that didn't belong to me in which I was supposed to pick up passengers and take them where they wanted to go, for which they would hand over their hard earned money. My biggest fear, other than getting in an accident, was not knowing how to get where a passenger wanted to go. I initially found myself doing what I did during my high school football days, trying to avoid contact. A dispatcher would issue a call on the radio for a pickup at such-and-such an address, and drivers in the vicinity would respond. The dispatcher would then assign the pickup to a driver. I became quite adept at not answering the calls quickly enough.

The downside to that (there is always a downside, darn it) was not getting paid, so I sucked it up and started answering calls. To help get over my nerves, I made a game of it, imagining my dispatcher as a

Tony Rogers' Taxi License

fellow ham operator and my cab radio as the 2 meter rig I had in my car when I was a ham.

Bizarrely, I was more worried about not knowing directions than of being robbed at gunpoint. The cab I drove came equipped with a plexi-glass safety shield (thank you, Tony Rogers), but that wasn't the reason. The reason was that my fear of embarrassing myself was greater than my fear of getting killed. If Descartes drove a cab, he would revise his famous dictum to read, "I am excessively self-conscious, therefore I am."

I received compliments on my driving. One that stuck with me was given me by an old gentleman who was accompanied by his daughter or caretaker. Although he was very feeble, he had impeccable manners, and when we reached his destination he said, "Young man, you are a very good driver." Before he got out of the cab, he instructed the young woman accompanying him to leave a big tip. I was oddly touched by what he said. Most passengers barely noticed the driver.

Most of my fares came from radio calls but I also picked up passengers on the street. As I was dropping a passenger off one morning, a woman in her thirties got in the cab. She looked hurried. "Airport, please." I pulled away from the curb. I was in a section of town I didn't know well and wasn't sure how to get on the GW Parkway. I took a guess and made a wrong turn. "No, no, no," my passenger said from the backseat. "You took a wrong turn."

"I'm sorry. I'm new."

"I'm going to be late."

"What time's your flight?"

"I'm not going anywhere. I work at the airport."

"I'm sorry." I drove faster than usual on the twisting road and in my hurry missed another turn. The woman loudly exclaimed, "Oh, no! Not again."

"I'm sorry, I'm really sorry."

I glanced in the rearview mirror. She had slunk down in the seat, as if hiding from her boss. "I'm going to get killed."

After a ride that seemed eternal, I pulled up at the main terminal. She reached over the seat and handed me the fare. To my surprise, she had included a nice tip.

"I can't take this. Please. I won't even charge you. I'll eat the fare."

"No," she insisted, sliding out of the seat. "Take it. It's yours."

This was not as embarrassing as my Charlie Byrd in E flat incident, but it was in the ballpark. As soon as I got off my shift, I asked the dispatcher for directions to the airport. I didn't want the same thing to happen again.

One of the myths about driving a taxi is that you are your own boss. The myth fits into the romantic view of the open road; a car, no boss, and nowhere to go. Freedom.

Not true in general, I think, and definitely not true about cabs. Once a fare gets in your cab, he or she is the boss. You go where your fare wants to go. You can't say, "Sorry, sir, I don't feel like going to Takoma Park today. Anywhere else I can take you? Or maybe we'll just sit here awhile and enjoy the morning." On the other hand, once a cab is underway, a passenger is at the mercy of the driver however demonic. Who among us hasn't had a cab driver that rings every alarm bell in our bodies? My pitch: I may get lost on the way to the airport, but I am drug-free and presentable. You're welcome.

I was waiting at a taxi stand the next morning, thinking of how to end the short story I had started before I came to work. I tended to write in early morning. My imagination works best then. It was a story about a man on an exercise bike in the window of a high rise apartment as seen by someone in a neighboring building. It was about futility. "High Rise Health Addict In The Impersonal City," it was called. I was thinking about how to end the story when the radio sputtered, "246 Elm."

Cab radios can be hard to understand, but this call was clear, and I was near Elm. I answered the call and was given the fare.

End the story with the man still pedaling the bike going nowhere? End with the man giving up in frustration and pummeling the bike with a wrench (sorry, Herman)?

I turned the corner onto Elm, a quiet street of ranch houses, and found 246. After a minute of waiting, I tooted the horn. Gently, politely; just reminding you, I don't mean to be pushy. When no one came, I did what no experienced cab driver would do, I got out of the cab and walked to the front door. I rang the doorbell and turned to the side so I wouldn't alarm whoever came to the door and saw a strange man.

The door opened and I heard a shriek. Not a loud shriek, more a high-pitched expression of 'oh, no.' I turned to look. It was the woman I had driven to the airport the day before. I don't know which of us was more surprised. I scrambled for words. "Please, don't worry. I asked the dispatcher for directions at the end of the day, I know the way. I promise I'll get you to work on time." Her face did a swan dive from the high board. Jaw dropping and everything. Who could blame her? To her I must have looked like Freddie Krueger.

After her shriek, she was a perfect passenger. Calm in the back seat. Fat tip at the end. "Have a nice day." Even a smile. People surprise me. I would've said, no way am I getting in that guy's cab.

I ended my high-rise story with the man still on the bike going no-where. I submitted it when completed, and it was the first story of mine published.

CHAPTER NINETEEN

Jeff Joins The Navy

WHILE I WAS AWAY, my middle brother, Jeff, had dropped out of Harvard Medical School. He had entered medical school after graduating with honors from Dartmouth but decided after a year and a half that the practice of medicine was not for him. It endeared him to me. While I was floundering as a teenager, he was perfect, or so it seemed.

After he dropped out, he came to Bethesda to see Mother and Dad. He said he had an announcement to make. I went to the house to see him. When I arrived, Dad was still on the golf course. Jeff and I sat in the room off the living room where the ping-pong table had been. The room had been renovated into a comfortable sitting room, and the living room into a formal room for entertaining.

Jeff and I share a family resemblance, except that he has a more athletic build and I am better looking (family joke, not to be taken seriously). He looked fit.

"How was Paris?" he asked.

"Great. It was hard to leave."

"Why did you?"

"I told Dad I was still sorting that out. I had run out of reasons to stay, for one thing. How about you? Tough decision to leave medical school?"

Jeff can sound gruff when he's uncomfortable with a subject. "Yeah. I chose medical school because I've always liked science, which isn't the same thing as practicing medicine, I learned."

"Sounds like me and engineering. Do you have any idea what you'll do now?"

"That's what I came down to tell Mother and Dad. I'm joining the Navy."

"No kidding?"

"I told Mother when I arrived. I'll tell Dad when he gets home."

Dad arrived shortly after, fresh from the golf course. He looked invigorated. He gave Jeff a big smile and offered his hand. "How are you, Jeff?"

"Hi, Dad."

The three of us were approximately the same height. "I'm going to change my clothes. Be right down."

Jeff and I stood there somewhat awkwardly. Or, I felt awkward. Jeff always seemed more comfortable than I. It was one of the things I envied about him. There were times growing up when he was anything but comfortable, and he could be stubborn, very stubborn, but most of the time, he took things in stride.

He and I went to the kitchen to see if Mother could use some help preparing dinner. "Can we help?"

"If you two could set the table, that would be terrific."

"Of course," Jeff said.

The heavy silverware had come down from our grandmother. As we set the table I asked Jeff, "How did Mother take your news?"

"She seemed thrilled. But you know Mother, she seems thrilled about everything."

"You're following in Dad's footsteps. She must like that."

"I knew I'd get drafted, so I chose the Navy. I have very mixed feelings about Vietnam."

"Dad and I almost come to blows about it. I don't think he believes everything he says. He's so darn argumentative."

"Come on, Tony. You know Dad. Challenge him, and it's to the death."

"Why is he like that?"

Jeff shrugged. "He's a competition addict."

"It doesn't bother you as much as it bothers me. Why?"

"You tell me. You two rub each other the wrong way. I don't know why."

"You have more in common with him than I do, so he doesn't have as much to complain about with you, number one. And number two, you have a more easygoing personality than I do."

We finished putting the silverware and glasses on the table.

"Is that what you think?"

"Easygoing may not be the word. No Rogers is easygoing. Fewer things bother you, how about that?"

"Again, not true."

"Okay, you don't show it as much as I do."

"True. You have no skin. Not a thin skin, no skin."

Is that how he saw me? I didn't see myself that way. Mother came into the room carrying a plate of sweet rolls. "Everything ready? Good. After Bill has his drink, we'll sit down."

When my parents redid the rec room into a family room, they also installed a bay window in the living room, looking out at the backyard. My mother had landscaped the backyard into more than a play area. A terraced stone wall formed a small patio sheltered by trees near the bay window. Very pretty, very Mother.

Dad came downstairs dressed in pressed slacks and a sport coat, his thin blond hair still wet from the shower. He fixed his drink and took a seat on the curved sofa in the bay window. For a few moments, he seemed lost in a sense of physical well-being. "Chilly on the course today. Good sun, though."

"How have you been, Dad?" Jeff said.

"Very good. How about you?"

"No regrets."

"Why would there be?"

"I don't know. Dropping out of med school is a big deal."

Dad contemplated the ice in his drink. "You had your reasons."

"I know. But it was painful."

Dad bristled, not at Jeff but about an abstract point he wanted to make. "Never second-guess yourself, Jeff. It shows a lack of self-confidence. You had your reasons. That should be your position."

I sat at my usual place looking out at the front lawn, Dad at the head of the table on my immediate left, Mother at the other end, Jeff across from me. I instinctively expected Dad to harangue me about grades or lack of enthusiasm on the playing field. How indelible teenage impressions are! It was a relief, in a way, that Dad and I now argued about Vietnam instead of me.

He dug in. After a moment he stopped eating and looked at Jeff. "You have something to tell us?"

"I'm joining the Navy, Dad."

Dad forked his mashed potato. "Is that right?"

"Are you happy?"

"Proud."

Mother beamed.

Dad added, "Not much of a Naval presence in this war compared to some. Still important, though."

"What do you think will happen, Dad?" Jeff said.

Dad put down his fork. "Nixon wants to wind down the war. You'll still have time to serve."

"That sounds like years to me," I said.

"We discussed this, Tony. Dick doesn't want to commit to a timetable."

"Sounds like years to me."

Dad's tone changed to metal. "You don't give up, do you?"

"He doesn't have a plan to end the war. He hopes to wind it down. I hope to be heavyweight champion of the world."

"I'm tired of your cheap criticisms, Tony. You haven't paid the price. Dick's trying to become president. He wants to end the war. What's your plan?"

"Admit our mistake. Withdraw."

"That's not a plan. That's surrender."

"It's an admission of reality. We shouldn't have gone in, we can't win. We should get out."

Jeff in his Navy dress white uniform, 1968

"Don't you understand? If we do what you say, we'll look weak and helpless in the eyes of the world."

"That's a reflection of Nixon's fears. He's mortally afraid of not being considered tough."

Dad rose out of his chair. He sputtered, then exploded. "How the hell do you know what's going on in Dick's mind? Among your other invisible talents, are you a mind reader?"

"Dad, calm down. Nixon's running for president. I have a right to criticize him. Everyone does."

Dad hovered half in, half out, of his chair. Jeff had been silent as the argument built. Now he said to me, "You do have a right to criticize him, but Dad's point is that you are criticizing from the sidelines."

"I know that," I shot back. "But isn't that true of all voters? I'm a voter, I have a right."

"Of course you do," Jeff said firmly. "But cool it."

Dad lowered himself back into his seat. "I thought you would have learned more as you were growing up, Tony. You had a front row seat."

"I shouldn't have gotten off on this tangent," I said. "Jeff had an announcement to make, and I, as usual, got in the way."

Mother sighed in relief, and her shoulders lowered. "I think it's wonderful what you're doing, Jeff."

"Thanks, Mother."

"I do too," I chimed in.

"And you know how I feel." Dad's voice was calm again. Order had been restored, and he still occupied the head of the table.

I lingered longer than usual after dinner to talk to Jeff. Mother and Dad had gone to bed and we had the family room to ourselves.

The TV was on with the sound turned down.

"I thought you and Dad were going to have a food fight tonight," Jeff said.

"It happens a lot."

"Over Vietnam?"

"Yeah. And Nixon. I hate him."

"Really?"

"You don't?"

"He's got some good ideas."

"Come on, Jeff. Remember, 'You won't have Nixon to kick around anymore'? The guy's self-pitying and paranoid."

"Did you feel that way when he used to come to our house?"

"No, but I wasn't paying attention. Girls, ham radio, and rock and roll. Nixon was just a shadow in the background."

"Well, if he gets elected, let's hope he does have a plan to end the war. I talked to the recruiter and they need personnel for their hospital ships off the coast of Vietnam. I may be assigned to one because I have some medical school training."

"How do you feel about that?" I asked.

Jeff shrugged. "Could be interesting."

I was tired of fighting with Dad. I didn't come back from Europe to fight with him. But something about him set me off almost every time I was with him. It wasn't a lack of charm, grace, or wit. And I certainly recognized what he had done for the country. As I analyzed it, what set me off was that Dad was competitive with his children, especially me and Dale, but on occasion Jeff and Doug, and even with Mother when there was no one else around to argue with. That wasn't the father I wanted. I was paying him back by fighting with him.

I wasn't going to win because he was my father and cared more about winning then I did, but I could make him work to win. The war provided a topic we both felt fervently about but didn't need to take personally. Neither of us could foresee how soon the topic would become personal. Neither of us could foresee that soon Dad would be the secretary of state.

Bill Rogers and Richard Nixon, 1969

CHAPTER TWENTY

Secretary Of State

AFTER NIXON WON the election but before his swearing in as president, an inaugural gala was held at the National Guard Armory. When Dad's State Department limousine complete with security detail reached the armory, we joined a long queue of limousines creeping around an oval driveway to get to the entrance. We moved no more than a few feet at a time, but each time we moved, the security man in the front seat would talk into his sleeve and say, "We just moved one car length forward. Can you see us?" To which the security man waiting in plain sight at the entrance would reply, "I see you." This went on car length by car length until we reached the entrance. I had the impression that the security guys just liked talking on their radios. Which I could identify with.

Two days later, after the inauguration, inaugural balls were held in six different locations. The president and first lady attended each one. What I remember most about the ball our family attended was meeting Spiro Agnew, the newly sworn in vice president. My immediate, strong, visceral reaction was similar to what I had felt when Joseph McCarthy came to our house many years before. Agnew was a crook, McCarthy was a thug. They each made my skin crawl.

Early in Nixon's term, Secretary of Defense Mel Laird announced "Vietnamization," the secret plan to end the war. "Peace With Honor,"

President Nixon dubbed it. Slowly turn the war over to the South Vietnamese, with the operative word being "slowly." This seemed to anti-war people like me to be nothing but an attempt to defuse the anti-war movement while continuing the war indefinitely. I was incensed.

I became used to seeing my father on TV while he was at Justice, but that was as nothing compared to now. He seemed to be on every night at the beginning of the new administration. Mother invited my wife and me to dinner soon after Dad took office, and I was watching the news on the family room TV while we waited for Dad to get home. On TV he was saying a few impromptu words to reporters outside the State Department. I had never seen him so nervous. He was visibly shaking. As I watched, I became aware of someone standing in the doorway behind me. It was Dad, watching me watching him. An early meta-moment.

Dad pushed himself off the doorjamb. "How'd I do?" he asked.

"You looked nervous."

"I was terrified. I have a recurring nightmare I'm taking a law school exam I didn't prepare for. That's how I felt today."

Two qualities kept a man of considerable ego like my father from taking the limelight too seriously. One was that he really and truly considered himself a public servant, the other was his self-deprecating sense of humor.

At a dinner in his honor hosted by the ambassador from Iran (the US and Iran were friends at the time), Dad was praised by the ambassador for staying cool under pressure. When the ambassador sat down after making his toast, Dad rose and thanked him for his kind words. "But I have to make one correction. I'm not cool under pressure, I'm numb."

Dad didn't shun the limelight, but he didn't seek it either, unlike, say, his nemesis, Nixon's national security adviser, Henry Kissinger. Kissinger was a familiar type in Washington, a man whose ego hung on every word uttered about him. Kissinger believed that conspiracies constituted the missing dark matter that scientists seek and—poor Henry—believed that most of the conspiracies were aimed at him. His conspiratorial mutterings about my father, whispered in the receptive ear of Richard Nixon, had the desired effect, but even Nixon eventually got fed up with his meddling, according to H.R. Haldeman, Nixon's chief of staff (see *The Haldeman Diaries*). After Dad died, Kissinger wrote my mother a long letter of apology for the way he had treated Dad. Two problems: it was a little late for maximum effect since Dad was dead, and, second, my mother was in the final stages of a long, slow dementia and understood not a word.

My mother was a bellwether about people. She rarely spoke ill of anyone. One exception was Kissinger, whom she didn't trust for a second. To hear her talk about him was akin to hearing her say "oh, shit," instead of "hell's bells."

In February, 1969, the Vietcong killed 1,140 Americans in a major offensive against American bases. By April, over 33,000 Americans had died in the war, more than died in the Korean War. American college campuses were increasingly restive. So was I.

Through friends, I met David Hawk and Sam Brown, two young men who were planning monthly protests against the war, to be held in cities across the country. I said I would participate in the marches. I told them their plan to hold marches every month was the key. Relentless pressure. Nixon had to feel that it wouldn't let up.

By summer, the Vietnam Moratorium, as it came to be called, took on a life of its own. It became apparent how much pent-up anger and resolve existed, especially but not solely among the young. Nixon announced a token withdrawal of 25,000 troops. Half a million troops remained in Vietnam.

I joined Dad by the pool in late August. I wanted to warn him what was coming. "The marches are going to be huge," I told him.

"How big?"

"I don't know. A hundred thousand in Washington."

"You think so?"

"I do."

Dad seemed thoughtful. He didn't snap a retort. "You may be right."

I wasn't used to him agreeing with me. I figured I hadn't expressed myself clearly or he hadn't heard me correctly. "Campuses are boiling."

"I sense that."

"Does the president understand?"

Dad never spoke of his private dealings with Nixon. "Hard to tell."

"I mean, 25,000 troops is good, but if he thinks that'll satisfy the protestors, he's wrong."

Dad was stretched out on a lounge chair. He turned his head toward me. "Have you considered he might be doing it because he wants to wind down the war?"

"I'll believe it when I see it."

Dad closed his eyes against the sun. "You are a harsh critic."

The humidity was high but not as high as mid-summer, when bones wilt and the skin cannot breathe. "About the war, yes."

"I wish I had that luxury. Nothing seems clear-cut from Foggy Bottom. The complications are endless."

He wasn't fighting back. Something must be wrong.

"Are you okay?" I asked.

"Sure. Why?"

"You don't seem like yourself."

Dad never seemed burdened by his work. That was one thing I admired about him. He never talked about how heavy his load was. To hear him sound subdued was disturbing.

"This isn't World War II with clear good guys and bad guys. Dick means well. Give him time."

"Dad, I should tell you that I'm planning to march in the protests. It's nothing personal."

"Are you sure it's not?"

"Yes, I am."

"Do me one favor. Stay away from the press. It would be very embarrassing for me if word got out that my son was marching."

The first march was scheduled for October 15. As the date approached, the organizers seemed daunted and exhilarated by the numbers expected to march in cities around the country. Busloads of people were coming to Washington from out of state. The networks planned live television coverage. The protesters would march down Pennsylvania Avenue and congregate on the Mall. The Washington police cancelled all leaves to handle the crowd. There was a heady feeling as those involved realized the power they had unleashed.

A few days before the march, Mel Laird's son publicly announced that he would join the protests. If I let it be known that I, too was marching, then both the secretary of defense's son and the secretary of state's son would be on record against the war. A powerful message.

I contacted the organizers and asked them what they thought. They were ecstatic. "We can set up a press conference for you two. The press eats up this sort of thing."

I felt a surge of power. To have an impact, maybe influence the course of the war. Wow.

"I need to think about this," I told them. "I'll get back to you."

"Okay, but hurry. We've only got a few days until the march, and it'll take time to arrange the press conference."

Dad would be livid. "Do me one favor, stay away from the press," he had asked. I owed him a head's up. I reached him at home. "Is this a bad time?" I asked.

"No. What's on your mind."

"Did you hear that Mel Laird's son has spoken out against the war?"

"I did. Mel isn't happy."

"I'm thinking of doing the same thing, and I want to hear your reaction."

A long pause. "Don't. It would embarrass me and make my job harder. I ask you as my son not to do it."

"The organizers of the march said they would arrange a press conference for the two of us. They were thrilled at the prospect."

"Did you tell them you'd do it?"

"I told them I'd get back to them. That's why I'm calling. I didn't want to do this without telling you first."

Dad sounded deeply concerned, but not angry. "Please don't. For my sake, don't do it."

"I want to lend my support to the antiwar effort. My statement might encourage others to protest."

"I know you're sincere. But if you join Mel's son, it would complicate things for me within the administration."

Dad's tone moved me. There was none of the combativeness he usually displayed, none of the competitiveness my opinions seemed to bring out in him.

(Years later, I learned that Dad and Mel Laird had been relative doves within the administration. The main hawk had been Henry Kissinger. Only then did I understand what Dad had meant when he said my going public would complicate things for him within the administration. It is a mark of his loyalty and sense of public service that he never revealed to me that he was urging a speedier pullout, even though doing so would have made me his ally instead of his antagonist.)

I didn't know what was the right thing to do. I needed advice. A family friend who knew both Dad and me (and was on the board of the Newport Jazz Festival which is how we met) had a wisdom I lacked. I called him at home and explained the situation. We weighed the pros and cons. Then, he offered this,

"I think you have to weigh the actual good you would do against the harm to your father. Would you and Laird's son making a joint statement bring the war to an earlier end? Probably not. My guess is it would make a splash for two or three days, then be forgotten. Weigh that against the harm to your father. Making a public statement wouldn't cause him permanent damage, but it would be embarrassing. And you have to consider what it would do to your personal relationship with him. How important is that to you?"

I slept (fitfully) on my decision and woke up leaning against going public. I needed to talk to Dad one more time before making up my mind.

"I'm leaning against going public," I told him. "But I *am* going to march."

"I understand. Just please avoid the TV cameras. I am grateful to you, Tony."

The next day I told the organizers what I had decided. They were very disappointed. "It would have a major impact." For a moment, I second-guessed myself. "Sorry," I told them.

The crowds began to appear early on the 15th. Many who had come from out-of-town camped out on the Mall. When I arrived downtown, I was stunned by the magnitude, and the march itself hadn't officially started. The mood was both festive and somber. These were determined people, every demographic, thousands and thousands of them. The crowds became so dense that the nation's capital seemed to have no roads, only people. We started to move down Pennsylvania Avenue. As we moved, our feeling of power grew. Except for the lack of burned out cars and barricades, it reminded me of Paris in May 1968.

The Mall was already full of people when the line of march reached it. Incredible sight. Everywhere you looked, people. No nook or cranny people-free. We The People.

One went where the crowd wanted to go, and I ended up on the grassy slope at the base of the Washington Monument. From it I could see down to the Lincoln Memorial and up to the Capitol. During the assassinations and race riots of the sixties, I had felt ashamed of America; on the Mall on this Moratorium Day, I felt proud.

Someone called my name. I had purposely come alone so as to not attract attention. "Tony! Tony!" A man my age was pushing his way through the crowd to get to me. As he got near I recognized a former classmate of mine from high school. He caught up with me. "Tony, what the hell are *you* doing here?"

"Protesting, like everyone else."

"Does your dad know you're here?"

"Of course. Good to see you, Mike."

"Same here. Wow." Mike was a head shorter than most in the crowd. If I hadn't been standing on a slope, he wouldn't have been able to spot me. He grabbed my arm. "We gotta get you on TV. My buddy works for WTOP. Come on." Mike tugged me towards one of the many TV cameras covering the march.

"Can't do it, Mike."

"Why not? This is huge. You and Mel Laird's son. Amazing."

"That's why I can't do it."

"You've got to, Tony. You're here because you want to end the war, aren't you?"

"It's complicated, Mike. Conflicting loyalties."

Mike pulled my arm. "Come on."

"Sorry." I wrenched free and ducked into the crowd. Mike tried to follow, but I managed to lose him.

I watched the march on TV that night. To say my feelings were mixed is an understatement. I felt awed by the size and spirit of the march, which only partially came through on TV, but I felt guilty for not speaking out. I felt even guiltier when Dad called to thank me. "Thanks for avoiding the press. I wasn't sure if you would."

"Actually, it was a close call. Someone I knew recognized me and tried to drag me in front of the cameras."

"Thank you again. I hope you feel okay with your decision."

That is the question. No matter how much I had assured Dad that my marching wasn't personal, it felt personal as I watched on TV that evening. I felt as if I had marched against my father, not against the war. For all the ups and downs of our relationship, for all our mutual misunderstandings, I hated, absolutely hated, the feeling of having betrayed him. Yet I hadn't betrayed him; I had satisfied my conscience by marching, while honoring his request to stay private. Why then did I feel like a traitor?

And then I got angry at him. If he had understood me when I needed understanding, if he had ever bothered to learn what kind of person I was instead of seeing me as the person he wanted me to be, I wouldn't feel so conflicted. But Tony, I argued, he's been understanding about this whole protest thing. Take note and stop whining.

Two hundred and fifty thousand people had marched in Washington, over a million around the country. It had been the biggest one-day protest in the history of the country.

CHAPTER TWENTY-ONE

Violence

THE PLAN OF THE protest leaders was to hold monthly marches, but before the second march took place, Vice President Spiro Agnew gave a speech that tore into the TV networks for their biased coverage of the antiwar movement. All three networks covered Agnew's speech live; *none* of the three networks covered the second protest march live. I was shocked. Could the press be manipulated so easily? Was the collective skin of the press so thin? Without the magnifying effect of the press, the protests stood little chance of persuading the administration.

The second march was even bigger than the first. Keep up pressure month after month and the president would have to listen was the original plan, but the leaders of the Moratorium became discouraged and failed to follow through. No more massive marches took place in D.C. The Mall reverted to tourists. I was even more shocked by this loss of will than by the caving in of the networks. I began to understand how dictators gain power. If intimidation was that easy, anyone could do it.

My brother did indeed go to Vietnam. He was assigned to a hospital ship off the coast of Vietnam, where the wounded were helicoptered for treatment. Jeff had mixed feelings about the war going in. His service removed the question marks, and he became virulently antiwar, writing passionate letters to Dad explaining how differently the war looked from the theater of war than it did back in the States. Dad visited Saigon during the war, and Jeff was given permission to go ashore and meet with him. The photo of their meeting is almost surreal. Pictures of secretaries of state greeting military personnel during a war are not unusual, except when one of the men is your father, the other your brother.

Nixon was shrewd. Over the course of his first year in office he withdrew enough troops to create a sense of movement toward peace, while continuing to bomb the North Vietnamese. It wasn't known at the time, but we had also been bombing Vietcong bases across the Cambodia border for months.

I was getting restless and thinking of moving. Part of the reason I had chosen the D.C. area to live in after Paris was to see if I could get along with Dad better now that I had gained self-confidence. I had the feeling that experiment was reaching its natural conclusion.

In the early spring of 1970, I joined Dad by the pool for what turned out to be the last time before I moved. The sun wasn't strong and the tarp hadn't been removed from the pool yet, but Dad jumped at any chance to sunbathe. I sat in a lounge chair in street clothes.

"This pool is the best thing Adele and I ever did."

"It's nice. We lived in poverty while I was growing up. We didn't have a pool."

He chuckled. "Adele and I sought to deprive the four of you."

"You succeeded."

"What are you going to do for a living after you get tired of driving a cab?"

"I'm still debating that."

"I didn't have the luxury of finding myself. I had to work every second. Did I tell you I sold Fuller Brushes during college?"

"Often."

"And waited on tables during the summers?"

"That too."

"Not a second to think big thoughts or wonder where I was going."

"I'm fortunate."

"Did I tell you I was offered a job as manager of the restaurant where

I worked? When I was debating whether to go to law school. The owner said I could become a part-owner if it worked out. I had so little money it was very tempting. I'm glad I chose law school."

"History would have been altered if you had taken the job."

"I'll say."

"I'm thinking about fate."

"That's the kind of thing I don't think about. I deal with things as they are. It has taken me far."

"What did you aspire to when you were growing up in Norfolk?"

"Getting out of Norfolk."

"Not government? Not law?"

"Debating appealed to me so I thought about law as a possibility. Or journalism. But mainly I wanted out."

"Are you satisfied with the ways things turned out for you?"

"That's the kind of thing I don't think about. I know I'm lucky, if that's what you mean."

"I mean, if you had your life to do over, would you do the same thing?"

He shook his head. "Don't know. I know I'm lucky, that's all."

We lay in the sun for a while without speaking. There was enough of a breeze that I didn't feel hot even in street clothes. How strange to sunbathe beside a tarp-covered pool in street clothes beside a man you used to be afraid to talk to. I closed my eyes.

His voice seemed to come from a distance. "Tony, what do you think would happen on college campuses if we invaded Cambodia?"

I raised my head just enough to see him. "I think all hell would break loose."

"That's what I think, too."

"Nixon's not going to do that, is he?"

"Just wanted your opinion. Thanks."

He had never asked my opinion about the war before, knowing how I felt. The fact that he had now worried me. The administration must be considering an invasion or he wouldn't have asked.

I was horrified by the prospect, but moved that he wanted to know my opinion. It was so rare.

On April 30, Nixon announced that we were invading Cambodia and that 150,000 more men would be drafted. All hell broke loose on campuses, culminating May 4 in the killing of four Kent State students by the National Guard. A picture of one of the students lying dead on the ground while a young woman cried out in horror became the iconic photograph of the antiwar movement.

—⟞⟝—

My then-wife and I moved to Boston in the summer. I liked Boston when I was in law school. It seemed more like a real city than Washington. I was sick of being at the epicenter of politics during the Nixon era, tired of a front-row seat.

There is always a psychological motive to what we do. When I moved to Paris I sought distance to sort out who I was versus who I was supposed to be if I were to be a good Rogers. I had returned to Washington more independent but still seeking my father's approval, still hoping he would say he liked who I was. In other words be the father I wanted to have. That was never to be, I now saw. We were too dissimilar. I couldn't hold that against him because that's who *he* was.

I had emulated Dad by getting a law degree, then distanced myself by moving to Paris. Success of a sort. But I was still seeking his approval. Time to permanently give up that quest. Let go of him. Don't turn your back on him but stop wanting something from him that he can't give. See him as he is, not as you want him to be. You want him to see *you* as you are, don't you?

Easy to say, painful to do, liberating when done.

—⟞⟝—

I liked the feel of Boston. Gritty enough to seem real, small enough to be manageable, and more European than most U.S. cities. The unpredictable streets and back alleys of Beacon Hill and the South End reminded me of Paris. I sought employment at Ellis Memorial, the South End settlement house where I had volunteered my third year in law school. My timing was good. They were looking for someone to supervise their nighttime drop-in center for teens. My hours would be four to midnight, five days a week. Perfect for me. I could write in the mornings—my preferred writing time—then go to work. The pay was meager but better than at the school in Paris.

This was the pre-gentrified South End. The streets and alleyways were downright dangerous at night. Castle Square, a large housing project, was a block from the settlement house. Old people got mugged on the streets with monotonous regularity. I quickly learned—because they bragged about it—that some of the teens who frequented the drop-in center were among the muggers.

The settlement house smelled old, in need of a good airing-out and a coat of paint. The drop-in center consisted of a first floor room with pool tables and soda-stained sofas, and a small third floor gymnasium with a basketball court. Half of the teens who frequented the drop-in center were black, half were white. About half were heroin addicts, hence the muggings.

I didn't know enough to be scared at first. After all, I was a well-meaning liberal, and had managed a lunch room in a Catholic school in Paris. Same thing, right? Soon enough my stomach was in knots every time I drove to work. I parked as close to the settlement house as I could and walked with my eyes sweeping the streets like radar, especially when I walked back to my car at midnight. The nominal leader of the black teens, a smart, intimidating eighteen-year-old named Wayne, pronounced me "okay" after he got to know me. I think that was the only reason I didn't get mugged. (I should add that Wayne followed that up with, "but you're white and if fighting ever breaks out in here, you're in trouble.")

To see Wayne was to freeze. Broad-shouldered with a merciless glare, he looked like the menacing figure in a dark alley nightmare. When you talked to him, however, his intelligence quickly became obvious. He wrote poetry. Good poetry. He was also a heroin addict, which he spoke openly about. He had a fatalistic laugh when he talked about shooting up, a "isn't this a crazy way to live?" kind of chortle.

He wasn't alone in how openly he talked about his addiction. Nor about what it was like growing up in the projects. Most of the kids, both black and white, lived with their mothers, the fathers being long gone. The stunning thing was how many of the kids transcended their upbringings. One of my favorites, a black kid named Poncho, became a Boston firefighter, yet he came from exactly the same kind of family as Wayne. I wished I understood why the difference, assuming it had something to do with their mothers, but I never got to know their home lives well enough.

I asked Wayne why he used heroin. He said it was the only pleasure he got out of life. He knew he'd end up dead or in jail by the time he was twenty-one. That answer was echoed by others. They said it with a touch of bravado, which made me suspicious, and a touch of fear, which made me believe them. They weren't lying, as it turned out.

I wore blue jeans to work, which made me the subject of ridicule from the black kids. Wayne put it this way, "You're rich, right?"

"Not at all. What makes you say that?"

"You got a law degree, don't you?" (I hadn't hidden that fact).

"I do, but I'm not rich."

That flummoxed him a little, but he recovered quickly, "If I were rich, I'd buy the best clothes I could find. Fancy stuff. Showoff clothes. Jeans are for poor people."

One night, Wayne asked me to read his poetry. I said sure, but reminded him I wrote prose. He didn't care, I was a writer. He proudly, apprehensively, showed me some poems. To my relief, I could honestly tell him his poems were good. He had a natural feel for language, a good sense of structure. He tried to downplay how thrilled he was when I told him.

I wasn't sure what to tell him about the content. More than one of the poems was about killing honkies. I decided to ignore the threats and treat it as poetry, which I think was the right decision. From then on, he showed me everything he wrote.

I had no doubt whose side Wayne would be on if a fight between blacks and whites broke out, but after I got to know him I wasn't scared of him. I was plenty scared of a sixteen-year-old named Robert who had just served two years in a secure juvenile facility for fracturing the skull of his grandmother when she caught him stealing from her. Robert was the scariest guy I have ever known. He had conscienceless eyes, without a trace of recognition that other human beings exist. He looked on people as prey. The only eyes I have seen as soulless as his were the eyes of the dead girl lying on a gurney in my Missouri friend's funeral parlor.

Robert didn't have to wait until he was twenty-one to wind up in jail, he made it at eighteen, beating Wayne by three years.

In spite of how menacing these guys were, I learned when they let down their guard that none of them had crossed the bridge over the Massachusetts Turnpike and gone to Newbury Street. The settlement house was one block away from the Massachusetts Turnpike, which sliced the city in two. Newbury Street, Boston's fanciest shopping street, was four blocks on the other side. They had never seen it. When I asked them why, they had no answer, but reading between the lines, I believe they were saying it wasn't their turf. None of them would say so—not even Wayne, who was honest about his fears—but I sensed that these tough guys feared streets they didn't control.

They also feared the police. Most of the black members of the group had repeated run-ins with the police, which they described in painful, consistent detail. Getting beaten in the back of a paddy wagon was a rite of passage. Even a soft-spoken, non-addict, non-thief like Poncho had his stories about been picked up for no reason and beaten. Most of the beatings ended with being let back out on the street, not to arrest. It was intimidation, pure and simple.

I got into one fight while I worked there. A seventeen-year-old named Paul, a nice enough but not to be trifled with guy, came to the settlement house door when we were closed. He was a tall, good-looking kid, whose girlfriend was with him. I think he wanted to impress her, because when I told him we were closed, he shoved me out of the way and barged in. What was a playful shove for him seemed like an assault to me and I took a swing at him. My punch landed on his cheek. It had all the effect of a gentle breeze, and I filed away a note in my mind that I should never ever strike a blow against anyone again the rest of my life. Paul's expression hardened, and he came at me with force. Unlike me, he knew how to fight. As I felt the difference between his shoving me and hitting me, I realized my mistake. He pounded me repeatedly in the face and started on the body.

I was about to black out. Strange how the mind works in extremis. Time slowed down, and I calmly tried to think of how I could get out of this. I remembered one of the guys demonstrating how he wielded a chair to ward off opponents in a fight. Out of the corner of my eye I spotted a metal chair. I grabbed it and held Paul off like a matador. Son of a gun, it worked! (Useful information for your next fight, grip the back of the chair tightly with both hands and hold the chair with the legs facing forward.)

Paul seemed bored with the whole thing. He motioned to his girlfriend and they took off. Only then, as I started to shake, did I realize how frightened I was.

The fight left me with a black eye and bruises. It also made me the butt of jokes in the drop-in center, as Paul told his story and word circulated. To my surprise, I gained prestige from the fight. There was ridicule, to be sure, a lot of pointing and snickering at my black eye, but it was the kind of ridicule you give one of your own.

A year after I started at the settlement house it was sold and I was out of a job. I'm amazed I didn't get an ulcer from my year there. My stomach hurt for weeks after the job ended.

A month after I stopped working at the settlement house, Paul was stabbed in a fight and almost died.

CHAPTER TWENTY-TWO

Exit State

ONE OF THE OBJECTS my siblings and I inherited was a map of the world showing all the countries my father visited as Secretary of State. Over sixty of them. The Vietnam War aroused anti-U.S. sentiments around the world. Home or abroad, Dad never traveled without State Department security. On August 1, 1969, as Dad was saying goodbye to Japanese officials on the Tokyo airport tarmac before flying to Korea, a knife-wielding man lunged at him. Dad's security detail tackled the man and wrestled the knife from him. Dad didn't tell me about the attempt on his life; I learned of it from the press. The AP quoted my mother: "We certainly were lucky. Next time we'll be looking in all directions." When I finally spoke to Dad, he downplayed the assassination attempt. "I was never in danger."

The State Department converted my parents' garage into a guard house, complete with a one-way window overlooking the driveway and round-the-clock protection. The security guards were armed with automatic weapons. Since I lived in Boston and rarely visited Bethesda, I imagined that they wouldn't recognize me as I drove up the driveway and would open fire.

My youngest brother wed during this tense period. Doug had met his fiancée, the daughter of the secretary of agriculture, at Dad's swearing

Bill Rogers in Paris with Richard Nixon (on podium) 1969

in. The wedding took place at the National Presbyterian Church across the District Line. The church is a somewhat forbidding structure with an enormous nave. Jeff and I were ushers. Given that the wedding was of two cabinet officers' children, a large number of dignitaries attended, and among the couples I escorted to their seats were John Mitchell, the attorney general, and his wife, Martha. Martha Mitchell had not yet established a reputation for bizarre behavior, but she seemed not in keeping with the other women in the church. There was coquettishness in her manner and showgirl in her looks. I offered my arm, which she gladly took. I was just doing my duty but John Mitchell glared at me as if I were trying to steal his wife. He glared at me all the way down the aisle. Spiro Agnew looked like a crook, John Mitchell looked like a hit man. What was Nixon doing surrounding himself with such people? And why was my suave, sophisticated father working for him?

I rode in Dad's State Department limousine after the service was over. A small reception was to be held at our house. Dad's limo was always preceded and followed by other security cars, even when not in a wedding procession. A State Department security agent rode shotgun in the front seat.

My mother had done the unusual: hired a cook to help with the reception. On the way home Mother suddenly exclaimed, "I forgot to tell the cook when to put the turkey in the oven." Mother did not like to make mistakes. She was gentle on the lapses of others, hard on her own. She also didn't like to ask others to do something for her. But wedding receptions were an exception.

She leaned forward. "Can you radio the house and ask the cook to put the turkey in the oven?" she politely asked the agent.

"Yes, Ma'am." The agent talked into his sleeve. I wish I could remember Dad's code name, but I can't. The conversation went something like this, and remember that this took place at the height of the Cold War. "Elysian Fields, this is Sweat Shop One. Please pass this message to the cook: put the turkey in the oven. I repeat: put the turkey in the oven."

On the assumption that the Soviets monitored all government communications and were hearing this, I imagined their consternation. "Put the turkey in the oven? What is the meaning of this? Arm the nuclear missiles in their silos and prepare to launch?" I imagined World War III breaking out because of my brother's wedding.

I was glad to be away from Washington during those corrosive years. Boston seemed saner. But good things happened, too. Dad authored the Rogers Plan for the Middle East, which traded land for peace and became the model for the two-state solution which remains U.S. policy to

Bill Rogers signs the agreement to end the Vietnam War, Paris, 1973

this day. Kissinger orchestrated Nixon's trip to China. And in January, 1973, Dad signed the Vietnam peace treaty in Paris, four years after Nixon became president, four years and thousands of deaths after Nixon promised he had a secret plan to end the war. Dad gave me one of the pens he used to sign the treaty. I have it in my study.

I thought back to the tension between us over Vietnam. How I regretted it. Fighting with him over sports and grades while I was in high school was one thing; fighting with him over war and peace had been of an entirely different order of magnitude. Less personal, more painful. The irony was that Dad had been a dove within the administration. He and Mel Laird had repeatedly urged restraint in contrast to the show-no-weakness, manly-man stance of Kissinger and Nixon. Escalate to force the North Vietnamese to the negotiating table had been the strategy, except that doing so prolonged the war for four unnecessary years. Peace With Honor had been the goal, but the result was that North Vietnam conquered the South two years after the signing of the peace treaty. A total failure.

Dad resigned in the fall of 1973, after Nixon won a second term. As the world knows, Nixon resigned in disgrace a year later.

—⚶—

After my siblings and I left home, Mother wrote letters to us each week. She continued this practice until 1995. Her letters from the years Dad was secretary of state total 600 pages. She typed them on carbon paper and sent one copy to each of us. Because the fourth carbon copy was fainter than the first, she rotated the copies so that no one would always get the faintest copy.

My sister assembled the letters from the State Department years and gave us each a bound copy. Here is an excerpt from mother's letter after Dad announced his resignation. It is dated September 1, 1973.

> I sort of feel like singing that old song, 'Free at last.' It feels good to be out of the administration. Too many creepy things.

Later in the same letter.

> Friday morning I went up to Woolworks to take the needlepoint to be put on the footstool for each of you. They said it would take about 2 weeks.

A few paragraphs later, she recounts a farewell party given Dad by his State Department staff.

> It made a very nice day to end a fascinating 4½ years. It has been an awfully tough time for Daddy—largely due to the lousy White House situation—but the actual work he has loved, and done superbly.....His integrity has meant so much to the other Foreign Ministers. Henry is going to have to reform to gain their respect. For they just aren't used to being lied to.

Then she writes about flying to New York immediately after Dad announced his resignation.

> Because Daddy is still in the line of succession they insist on guarding him until Monday night. I wanted us to fly up commercially, but they said please not to. So I guess we are going on our last trip on the jet star. Seems a fiendish waste of money for the gov., for I can't imagine anyone trying to hurt Daddy now that he is practically out. But the security men will feel better that way. And Daddy will enjoy one last trip. Not having the plane start the minute he boards is going to feel strange for a while to him. Not to mention carrying money again. And opening doors, etc. But fortunately Daddy will do it very gracefully, as he did when he left the Justice Department.

Excerpts from letters immediately prior to Dad's announcement:

> Right now (5 p.m.) Daddy has probably just finished with the President, handing in his resignation. For their appointment began at 4....It is a hard time for each. We heartily disapprove of much the Pres. has done lately...Yet they are old friends, and in many ways, good friends....For his part, the Pres. is mad at Daddy. He wanted him badly to become Attorney General again, and bail him out. When

Bill and Adele Rogers, 1973

Daddy refused, he has tried time and again, up to about a week ago, to get him to come in the White House and straighten it out for him, or to come as his lawyer and bail him out. All of those Daddy, thank heavens, refused to do. So he won't be leaving with love and kisses. The Pres. feels he has let him down.

Daddy did talk to the Pres. for nearly two hours. He is in such an upset state of mind you feel sorry, and apprehensive. And obviously so do they. He certainly needs help. But I just don't think he will let anyone help him in the right way. The Nixon we knew and admired seems at least temporarily lost.

After praising Dad's drivers at State and Justice, and saying how much she and Dad will miss his State Department staff, she ends with,

Goodbye to this very exciting chapter in our lives. It's been a great privilege.

The Rogers family at Lake Tahoe, c. 1988

CHAPTER TWENTY-THREE

Fake Smiles

AFTER DAD LEFT the government, the family started spending a week each summer at Lake Tahoe. A close friend of Dad's owned a compound on the Nevada side of the lake. It had been built by a rich, eccentric bootlegger, eccentric being defined here as one who keeps elephants on his property. The location was spectacular. The crystal blue waters of Lake Tahoe looked good at any hour but sunset lent a glow that entered the realm of magic. The compound included a main house and several guest houses, all made of rough stone. A tunnel with tracks ran from the basement of the main house to the boathouse. The tracks were used to transport bootleg liquor—an underground railroad of the bootlegging trade.

Mother and Dad loved Lake Tahoe. Dad loved the sun, Mother loved the natural beauty and being surrounded by family. As my siblings and I had kids, the gatherings got quite big. We couldn't all fit around the dinner table, so card tables were set up to enlarge it. Dad held forth as usual, provoking, jabbing, talking politics, bragging in his humorous, self-deprecating way. If an election were coming—and there was always an election on the horizon—he would go around the table and ask each person, young or old, who they thought would win. It wasn't acceptable to say you didn't know. You had to take a guess. Nor was it an idle pastime, Dad kept score. Mother, on the other hand, would go around the table and ask what the high point of the year had been for each of us.

Because the property was so spectacular, sightseeing boats included it in their itinerary. It was a strange feeling to be sitting by the lake and hear a voice over a loudspeaker describing you as part of the scenery. There was a nudist beach down the lake, and sometimes sunbathers from the beach would float by on inner tubes. Mother was birdwatching on the shore one day when a small craft full of nudists trolled by, not ten feet away. Mother softly exclaimed "Oh, my," in her genteel way, and strolled back to the house as if the only reason she were going inside was that she had her fill of birdwatching for the day.

My parents had a tradition of using a family photo on their Christmas cards. As Dad's prominence grew, so did their Christmas card list, eventually numbering in the thousands. People who were total strangers to my siblings and me would tell us, "We watched you grow up." Life through a one-way mirror.

The Christmas photos were a big deal to Dad. He put enormous stock in how people looked, looks being an important part of the impression a person made and the impression a person made being an integral part of getting ahead. When I first saw *Death of a Salesman*, my heart broke when Willy Loman said, "He's liked, but he's not—well liked." Dad came from that era, and our Christmas photos were a part of making sure we were all well liked.

We hated posing for the photos. He wanted us to look a certain way, sometimes telling us what clothes to wear. I dress drably. Have all my life. I had to wear a coat and tie to Sidwell Friends, and I wore the same gray tweed sports coat every day until I finally had no choice but to replace it. When I came home with a new sports coat, Mother couldn't help mocking me in her gentle way. "My, there's a little blue in it, isn't there, dear?" What I am saying is I dressed drably for the photos not out of spite but habit. One year, I must have been in my forties, Dad insisted I wear one of his sports jackets, which was a bright yellow. I have never worn yellow in my life, let alone bright yellow.

Lake Tahoe became the venue-of-choice for our Christmas card

Rogers family Christmas cards, (clockwise from left) *1949, 1955, 1988.*
Tony (bottom card, back row center) *is wearing the yellow sports jacket.*

picture taking. As the number of children grew, it became increasingly hard to fit everyone in. Elaborate preparations were necessary. Sit here, stand there. Turn to the right, turn to the left. Children became grumpy. Adults became sardonic. If you stacked the pictures and riffled through them like a pack of cards, you could watch our family perfect our fake smiles. The secret to a convincing fake smile is to chuckle as you smile. An anthropologist observing our yearly ritual wouldn't have known what to make of the "heh, heh, heh's" rippling down the rows when the photographer said smile. A chain letter of chuckles.

On a Christmas card somewhere in the middle of the stack, you will see me in my father's bright yellow sports jacket.

A cliche that is none-the-less true is that being a parent makes you appreciate your own parents more. When I married Tamara in 1977, my two older children, David and Veronica, came to live with us. Our son, Sam, was born in 1981. I saw with each of my three how challenging it is to raise children. I vowed to avoid the mistakes of Dad without overcompensating. I didn't have to avoid my mother's mistakes since she did not make any. My siblings and I used to grouse about what a hardship it is to be raised by a perfect mother.

Though Mother's competitiveness had softer edges, she was every bit as competitive as Dad. Few women born in 1911 earned a law degree. If born in a later era, she would have had a highly successful career, I have no doubt. I believe she decided early in their marriage to satisfy her competitiveness by aligning it with Dad's. Together they made a formidable team. Dad was devoted to her. I never saw them physically affectionate, but when Mother survived difficult surgery late in life, Dad quietly sobbed when he learned she was okay.

The main house at Tahoe had a stone porch overlooking the lake. I liked to sit there because it was in the shade. Dad preferred the vest-pocket size beach just below and to the right of the porch. A year or two after Nixon's resignation, I was on the beach watching David splash his cousin while Dad sunbathed a few feet away. The beach was only half a dozen sunbathers wide. I asked Dad a question that had been preying on my mind.

"Did you know about Watergate?"

His eyes were closed. "Not until Dick asked for my advice."

"What did you tell him?"

"To get everything out in the open."

"Too bad he didn't follow your advice. Unbelievable the damage he did. How do you feel about him now?"

Dad opened his eyes. "I never had a friend lie to me before." He sat up as if startled by something he had forgotten or had heard in the distance.

"Are you in touch with him?"

"No. The final straw was when he asked me to fire Haldeman."

"He asked *you* to fire Haldeman? *After* you resigned?"

"Yes."

"What did you say?"

"I told him to go to hell."

My father may not have been the perfect father for a son like me, but damn, he was a good man. Before Watergate, Nixon purportedly characterized Dad as one of the "toughest, most cold-eyed, self-centered, and ambitious men" he had ever known. I wonder what he thought of Dad after Watergate. Dad was one of the few men who served in the Nixon administration whose reputation wasn't tarnished by Watergate.

When Nixon died, Dad went to his funeral. Out of loyalty to the friendship they once had, he said.

As Dad sorted through his memories later in life, he spoke admiringly of Eisenhower, who, he believed, didn't get enough credit. He said little about Nixon.

Having let my father go, I no longer needed his approval to the extent I once did, especially when I was away from him. I always relapsed a little when I was at Tahoe. Which led, when his approval wasn't forthcoming, to the bitter fights of yore. Fortunately the fights flared and faded quicker than before.

Most of the time we got along noticeably better. Mutual respect was taking root.

There was no single turning point. He mellowed when his ambitions were fulfilled and he was back with his old law firm, which now carried his name. The practice of law suited his aggressive, hard-driving nature. He loved it. I grew less resentful of him as I concentrated on my children, and as I no longer looked to him for approval. No single turning point, just a gradual process of seeing each other as we were, not as we wished the other to be.

We did not talk about love in our family. It got confused with competition (Dad) and duty (Mother), but it was there. I took the love for granted until I was much older. Mother's love for her family was always apparent, even if she rarely used the word. Dad's was there too, in his constant haranguing us about getting ahead. Self-made men often see the world as made in their image, and Dad was no exception. He was trying to equip us for a world he saw as hostile. He once told me that people don't do what they're supposed to unless there's a threat of punishment hanging over their heads. When he said that (I was in my teens) I was appalled. It was antithetical to my view of the world. I believe that, on balance, people want to do the right thing. That was one of the main divides between Dad's view of life and mine, the other being that he viewed the world as competitive in its DNA. He breathed competition. His heart pumped competition. His rewriting of Descartes would be, "I compete, therefore I am." When I was able to step back and put our differences in perspective, I just accepted that we were different. Period.

Somewhere along the line, I believe he came to the same conclusion.

CHAPTER TWENTY-FOUR

Strong Women

How DOING WELL and doing good mix together in children of the same parents fascinates me. The oldest child traditionally feels parental expectations the most, but it gets complex when the oldest is a girl, born at a time when women were primarily expected to raise a family. Dad treated women as equal human beings but not as equal competitors, and Dale had to fight harder to win his approval. That may partly explain her drive. She became a professor, then Dean of Wellesley College, then President of Wheaton College in Norton, Massachusetts. Jeff and Doug are Yale-trained lawyers. Between the two, they have covered the gambit of the law: Legal Aid, public defender, private practice, U.S. attorney, city attorney. Doug devoted many of his years as a Legal Aid attorney upholding the rights of the disabled. He served as deputy disability coordinator for the 2008 Obama campaign. Jeff, as city attorney for Portland, Oregon, blocked the FBI's post-9/11 edict to have the Portland police question people of Muslim faith.

In my career as a hospital administrator, I spent fifteen years as director of operations for the MIT Medical Department and ran a veterans' hospital. Jeff pointed out to me when we drove to see Dad's birthplace years later that as Dad's oldest son I had been number two in birth order, but number one in his expectations. I hadn't thought of it that way. I had

Dale Rogers Marshall with Adele and Bill Rogers. The photo was taken when Dale was acting president of Wellesley College, 1987.

assumed Dale bore the brunt of Dad's expectations.

The four of us were talking on the stone porch at Tahoe one afternoon in the eighties. "Do you really like being here?" I asked Dale, who often said she did.

"Don't you?" Dale has the same tall, lean build as Mother.

"I feel the pressures I did growing up in Bethesda. The years in between vanish. Can't stand it."

"Tahoe is the only place I'm able to relax. I float on an inner tube and read, what could be better?"

Doug commented, "You read all the time anyway."

True. On Mother's eightieth birthday, the four of us took her to the Southwest, which she loved, and hired a guide to take us on a jeep trip into the beautiful Canyon de Chelly, which she hadn't seen. We stopped for lunch beneath a looming rock wall, an idyllic spot, an almost spiritual spot. Dale perched on a boulder and read a book while she ate her sandwich. I walked closer to look at the title. She was reading a book on the Swedish social welfare system.

"I'm not the only one," Dale responded to Doug. "We all read."

Doug scoffed, "I read 'Jack and Jill went up the hill' compared to what you read."

Jeff seemed puzzled. "Seriously, is Tahoe the only place you relax?"

"Maybe not the only place," Dale wavered.

"Ah, ha!" Doug said. "An indecisive academic, who ever heard of such a thing?"

Dale seemed momentarily nonplused. My brothers and I mock each other all the time. Dale joins in when she gets the joke, but her default position is serious, so there was the equivalent of a five second tape delay before her mock-mode kicked in. "Tahoe is the *only* place I relax," she declared decisively.

Doug nodded. "Good save."

The sun had been overhead, now it angled in from the west. I put my legs up on the stone railing. We could hear the kids playing on the beach. Mother was watching them for us.

"I relax best in a canoe," Jeff said, still mulling it over.

"How is that different than relaxing on an inner tube?" Dale replied, a little bit miffed from the mocking.

"Because I'm paddling. I expend energy."

"The point of relaxing is to not expend energy."

"Stop it you two," Doug said. He held an imaginary microphone in front of me. "Tony Rogers, how do you relax?"

"I don't. Anxiety at all times. Best be prepared. Seriously, do any of you feel like a teenager again when you're here? I get the same rush of imminent combat before dinner that I did at all our family dinners in Bethesda."

"I never felt that," Jeff said.

"You're joking."

"I'm not joking."

"Doug?"

"Never felt it. I'm joking. I felt it but laid low. Dale and you seemed eager to get into it with Dad. I never understood why."

"Because I couldn't get him to agree with me, even when I knew he did," Dale said.

"We didn't have family discussions, we had Supreme Court debates," I said.

"I hated those fights," Jeff said.

"You stayed out of them."

"I didn't see the point."

I remember one argument between Dale and Dad before Dale left home for college. Dad's work in the cause of civil rights was one of his finest achievements as attorney general. When Dale said that she thought women had suffered as much as African Americans, Dad was incensed. As always, part of his ire was that of a racehorse chomping at the bit before the starting gate opens, but part of it was heartfelt. "Africans were brought here in chains. In the course of an ocean crossing, they became sub-human. How can you compare that to women?"

Dale didn't relent. She didn't deny his point but didn't understand why he wouldn't concede a little of hers. "Women have been oppressed for as long as there have been men. In many countries, they still have no rights except through their husbands. Even in advanced societies, women are often second-class citizens."

"But they're citizens."

"Not until recently."

And so on. The irony is that Dad defended women when he wasn't arguing about them.

I have lived surrounded by strong women. You could place my wife, my sister, and my mother on a time-line as exemplars of progress towards women's rights. Each in her own way and in her own time was, or is, a powerhouse. My wife, who attended Radcliffe in the early seventies and is now a vice-president of Harvard, had to work twice as hard as a man to achieve her goals; my sister, who came of age fifteen years earlier at the dawn of the feminist movement, had to work four or five times as hard as a man to achieve her goals; and my mother, who came of age at a far different time but was equally qualified, was expected to subordinate her goals to her husband's. Each reflected her era, each affected her era. If one human being could point to another and say "I am more human than you," then inequality can be justified. Absent that, there is no excuse for it, certainly not over something like gender.

Dad was sixty when he left State. His only government role after that was chairing the space shuttle *Challenger* commission. He didn't appear on talk shows, rarely gave interviews. When I asked why, he said it was impossible to know what was going on inside the government once you leave office. "I had my time and now it's time for others."

Tony's family: (standing) *David, Veronica Rogers Everett, Sam*
(seated) *Victoria, Madeline, Carmela, Tamara, Anna on Tony's lap*

CHAPTER TWENTY-FIVE

Essences

In 1995, twenty-two years after Dad left State, I won the Capricorn Award from the Writers Voice of New York for a collection of short stories, *Bewildered, Harold Faced The Day*. The award included a prize of $1,000, which was the most I had earned for my writing. My stories had appeared in many literary magazines, which for the most part paid in copies. I didn't care. I was earning a living as a hospital administrator and writing on weekends. As long as I could write, I was happy.

The Writers Voice invited me to read one of the stories from my collection at the awards ceremony in New York. I hadn't read in front of a sizeable crowd before and I was nervous, especially since my children, my wife, and my parents would be there.

Dad hadn't come to see my band play, even when I was playing professionally, so for him to come to my reading touched me. My cynical side said it was because I had won something, my mature side said it was because he was past caring about winning and came to congratulate me. It is hard to accept love when you've steeled yourself against it. Dad had gained a little weight and walked a little slower, but at eighty-two his health was good.

Mother had been a walker all her life, and at eighty-four, still had a fundamental robustness. She had volunteered as a reading tutor in elementary schools until well into her seventies, first in suburban schools, then inner-city schools. We marveled at her stamina and grit. The last school she worked at was in a dicey area of Washington. The children wrote her adoring letters, which their teacher assembled into an album and presented to the family at my mother's memorial service.

The auditorium of the YMCA where the awards ceremony took place was full and the air stifling. I was wearing a blue blazer and a red tie, and sweating like a hot, nervous writer. I thought of standing next to Eisenhower worrying about body odor, I thought of Dad's yellow sports jacket, anything to keep my mind off the crowd waiting to hear my story.

I was introduced by the judge who had chosen my story collection for the award. Assuming he would say nice things about my writing, and knowing I would blank on what he was saying, I asked my wife to remember for me.

The judge introduced me, then it was my turn. I stood on the podium, feeling self-conscious about my red tie. I thanked the Writers Voice and the family members and friends who had come to the reading, then singled out my oldest son, David, who as luck would have it, had just published his first two short stories. He hadn't known I was going to do that and seemed pleased. He got a big hand.

The story I read was told in the voice of a very dedicated, slightly out-of-touch high school English teacher. The humor of the story came from the contrast between what was actually going on and what he thinks is going on. For reasons that escape me, audiences at readings tend to listen solemnly, and for the first page of my story there was dead silence. Not a peep of laughter. Not one. If the humor didn't work for the audience, the story would die an ugly death. I felt terrible. What to do? There was nothing to do except keep reading.

Midway through the second page of the story, the teacher quotes from a student book report about *Of Mice And Men* which compares Lennie to Forest Gump. When I read that line, the audience exploded with laughter. I don't use the word exploded figuratively. The sound was like a shotgun being fired. A switch had been thrown, permission had been granted to laugh, and from then on, the audience laughed at every line. They laughed even when the line wasn't funny. I felt as if I were riding a wave. I can see why comedians get addicted to hearing laughter. The lift reminded me of what I felt when my band played well.

As I rode the laughter, I became worried because I knew what was coming and the audience didn't. The teacher, who has fallen in love with the school's new speech therapist, becomes sure she is carrying a torch for an old flame, and preventively dumps her. A poignant ending. Would the audience go along with that, or would they be disappointed?

The laughter sputtered to a stop as audience members slowly realized they were laughing at stuff that wasn't funny. I detected bafflement at first, then resentment; how dare you do this us? The story ends with the teacher saying, "We have a new speech therapist. Her name is Sarah. She is attractive, but I've had it with speech therapists," and I had the crowd back again.

I stepped down from the stage to the congratulations of many. One woman said she especially liked me mentioning my son.

My father shook my hand and patted me on the arm. "Good job." My mother hugged me, "Wonderful, dear, absolutely wonderful." When I had a moment with my wife, I asked her what the judge had said when he introduced me, "As I predicted, I don't remember a word." "Me either," she said. "Sorry."

—∞—

To celebrate, my parents took us to one of their favorite restaurants, the Four Seasons. Everyone was in a good mood. Our children, who ranged in age from 14 to 25, were not used to fancy restaurants and seemed a bit awed. Mother and Dad seemed relaxed and happy. Tamara sat beside me. She had told me in the cab on the way over that I had done well. I was still on a high and couldn't tell.

Saigon had fallen twenty years before, and the Vietnam War had been in the news again. Midway through the meal, Dad started to reminisce. He started slowly, warming up to the subject. I detected no edge in his voice. He seemed in a mood to assess, to sum up. Normally I would have

Bill Rogers with Tony, c. 1995

been suspicious, knowing he was a wily debater who knew how to lull an opponent into complacency. For some reason, I wasn't this time. I was eager to hear what he had to say.

Eager, but as it turned out, unprepared. In talking about the deliberations inside the Nixon administration, he said, "I argued at the time that we should get our troops out as quickly as possible, but I didn't think the war was wrong. I do now."

It took a second for his words to sink in. "You think the war was wrong?" I echoed inanely.

"Yes. If I had been your age, I would have done what you did. I would have marched in the streets. You were right to protest."

The emotions of the night overwhelmed me. From the high of the award to hearing my dad say the war had been wrong and I had been right to protest was just too much for me, and to my chagrin, I found myself sobbing. It's against the rules to cry in the Four Seasons unless your stock portfolio has plummeted, and I was sure I would be thrown out by an indignant maître d'. My wife saw what was happening and gripped my arm. She later assured me that I cried quietly but it sounded like sobbing to me.

Even as I cried, my mind kept churning, and I was stunned by how fresh the pain of that era was. I had no idea that much pain had been trapped inside me all those years, no idea that protesting against my father had hurt so much. To hear him say he would have done what I did wiped away the years, wiped away most of the pain.

It's too easy to label that night as the turning point in our relationship, it was more of a culmination. Dad had gradually mellowed after he left government, and I gradually came to accept him. The process had taken years. But for me that night became the night it all came together, the night the mellowing and acceptance came to light. It gave the process a name, a face. A reference point.

Thank you, Writers Voice. Thank you, Four Seasons. Thank you, Dad.

Three weeks after the reading, my mother fell down a flight of stairs as she was hurrying to get ready for an event she and Dad were to attend. She hit her head at the bottom of the stairs and went into seizure. Dad rushed her to the hospital where she spent the night. She was released the following day. That night she had another seizure. Dad called 911. This time the hospital did not release her the next day.

I flew down and saw her at the hospital that afternoon. She was lying on her back and struggling to breathe. Each breath seemed to take enormous effort. I was horrified. I rushed to the nursing station and told a nurse to raise my mother's head. The nurse did and Mother's breathing eased. I say this as a former hospital administrator: if you have to be hospitalized, take someone with you who can act as your advocate and lookout. Hospitals are prime examples of what happens when an organization gets so complicated that communications break down. You need someone who can speak up for you, badger the staff if necessary, challenge the doctors.

Mother was never the same. Her brain had received an injury from which she never recovered. The deterioration was slow but inexorable. She lived for another six years. Near the end, she could only respond to simple questions and for the final year, not at all. I spent endless hours with her in the breakfast nook, looking out the bay windows at the backyard bird feeder, hoping a bird would come along and give me something to point out. "Look, Mother, a bird. A cardinal. Pretty, isn't it?" Most of the time, Mother stared blankly out the window.

The blessing in all of this is that Mother never lashed out, as often happens in dementia. The opposite happened: Mother got sweeter and sweeter. We said among ourselves that it was as if everything of Mother was disappearing except her essence. Layers of insider-Washington politesse and the patrician good manners she had learned from her mother were stripped away, leaving nothing but sweetness.

My siblings and I knew right away that the Mother we had known was gone forever. I realized that when I spoke to her on the phone after her premature release from the hospital. Her voice was sluggish, her normal enthusiastic inflections flattened. Alive, but gone. It was very hard to accept.

Once we realized the severity of her wounds, we set up a rotation so that one of the four of us was with her in Bethesda almost every weekend. Dad was profoundly grateful. He expressed his gratitude openly and often. It was touching to see the tenderness he showed Mother. We had never doubted that's how he felt about her, but he had rarely displayed his feelings so openly.

CHAPTER TWENTY-SIX

The William P. Rogers Building

As Dad's health failed and Mother's continued to deteriorate, I had to steel myself before my monthly visits and fight back tears after I left. Many a cab driver must have wondered why the middle-aged man in the backseat was sniffling and wiping his nose; allergies, perhaps? (None of the cab drivers got lost on the way to the airport.) But the monthly visits were also a time of reflection and joy. We would sit in the upstairs library watching CNBC with the sound turned down so that Dad could follow the stock market, and he would tell his stories, in many of which he was the butt of the joke.

"Did I ever tell you about the time I was flying over Africa when I was secretary of state and we hit bad weather?"

"I'm not sure. Why don't you start, and I'll stop you if I've heard it before." That became my standard reply, since he eventually repeated each story many times, and I didn't want to deprive him of the pleasure of telling them.

"We were flying over sub-Saharan Africa when we hit the worst air pockets I've ever experienced. The plane tossed so violently my security men looked terrified. Have I told you this before?"

"Yes, you have, but it's a wonderful story. Keep going. I want to hear it again."

Dad chuckled. "Well, everybody was gripping their seats and saying their prayers. In the midst of all this, I piped up and said, 'I'll bet this never happened to John Foster Dulles.'"

I laughed. "Great story. Did your security men laugh?"

"Are you kidding me? They were too scared." Dad chuckled again.

He told stories about his childhood, many of which I had heard throughout my life. He told them in the vein of a man putting the puzzle of his life together. He talked about going to live with his grandparents, but not about the pain he must have felt to have his beloved mother die, nor the pain of having her replaced by a stepmother he couldn't stand. He talked about the pump in the backyard of the house where he was born and about going outside in the bitter cold for water. He had talked about the pump so many times I considered it part of the family.

He only talked about his father in practical terms: for example, his father losing his job in the paper mill and starting his own insurance agency. He talked again about working his way through college selling Fuller Brushes, and about the job offer from the restaurant owner. There was no wistfulness in the retelling of these stories. I detected some pride, considerable humor, and humility at the great, good luck that had enabled him to use his potential to the maximum. He knew he was good at what he did, and occasionally he thought he was good at something he knew nothing about—spillover hubris—but never did he suffer from megalomania.

He was not a man for analyzing himself. He left motives to others. He was a man who had taught himself how to navigate the seas of life, not a man who wonders where the waves come from.

—⁂—

Dad had heart surgery in 1997. His recovery was painfully slow. I think he was dumbfounded at not being in control of his body. Dad had never talked about death, but after he recovered from the operation, he asked me to accompany him to Arlington National Cemetery to pick out a grave site for Mother and him. I drove him over Memorial Bridge on a bright day with plenty of sun. A stiff breeze made it feel cooler than it was. "Nice day," Dad said, peering out the windshield.

We were met at the cemetery by an official who would show us around. He climbed in the backseat and pointed the way. We got out of the car at each possible location and the official would tell Dad which famous people were buried nearby. "This is prime territory, near President William Howard Taft." Later, "This is an excellent location. You've got Hugo Black and a good view."

The cemetery is hilly and peaceful. Many of the plots overlook the Potomac and the monuments of D.C. We got out at one spot that had a particularly nice view. A plot was available near the top of the hillside. A pretty place.

"What do you think of this?" he asked me.

"Peaceful. Mother would like it."

"I agree. I think this is our choice," he told the cemetery official.

Papers were signed in the cemetery office, and we drove home in silence. Dad seemed no different than if he were heading home after a day at the office. We found Mother at the table in the breakfast nook, visiting nurse beside her, staring blankly out the window at the birds.

Dad had hip surgery in 2000. One too many operations. He had gone into the office two or three days a week until then. After the hip surgery he essentially stopped going. He was eighty-seven.

On a visit in late autumn I was walking by the upstairs library door and saw Dad sitting in the sun, his eyes closed, his white hair in disarray. He was so pale and there was so little substance to his body that the sun seemed to shine right through him. I entered the room to check on him. Even after he opened his eyes, I couldn't shake the feeling I had glimpsed his ghost.

His law firm had told him they were renaming the firm's building in his honor. The question became would Dad live long enough to attend the dedication ceremony.

His longtime assistant Marie, a resourceful and fiercely loyal New Yorker, coordinated the event. The first date had to be cancelled when Dad wasn't up to it. The second date was a week before Christmas, when it was my turn to be there.

Dad was in terrible shape all weekend. Complaining how weak he was, complaining about his food. He didn't think he could go on Monday. "We'll see, Dad, no need to decide now," I said. "I really don't think I can go," he insisted.

"Maybe you'll feel better on Monday, Mr. Rogers," his nurse echoed.

He would have none of it. If he couldn't control life and death, at least he could control whether he left the house or not.

Sunday night he was absolutely sure. "Call Marie and tell her it's off."

"It's too late to call, Dad. I'll call her tomorrow."

"No, call now."

"You don't know how you'll feel tomorrow. Let's wait and see."

The morning came. No go. He felt worse. I conferred with the nurse, who thought he could do it. So did Marie when I called her, although Marie thinks everything is doable.

We alerted the office that it might be off, but kept working on Dad. Crunch time arrived, and he had to make a decision. We got him out the door by dressing him in a suit and tie. Once dressed, he felt better. "Okay," he said.

We didn't give him a chance to renege. The law firm had sent their car, and we hustled him in the backseat. The vacant look in his eyes was that of a homeless man. The streets we passed looked familiar but I couldn't place them. Time stretched thin. He could still change his mind.

We neared his office. "Comb my hair, will you?" He handed me his comb.

He was gaunt, skeletal, shrunken, but he wanted me to comb his hair. "Sure, Dad."

I combed his hair. The hair of the man I had respected and feared all my life. His hair had so little substance by then it wouldn't stay down. I did the best I could.

We rounded the final corner. I could see his office mid-block, and Marie waiting by the curb with a wheelchair.

"We're almost there. Ready, Dad?"

He gave a slight nod.

The opening of the William P. Rogers Building, 2001 K St. NW,
Washington, D.C., December 11, 2000
Bill Rogers (center) is accompanied (to his left) by Marie Hunter,
his assistant for many years.

The car pulled up to the curb. "Okay, here we go."

I jumped out and we helped him into the wheelchair. His reluctance made him heavy to lift, yet he looked so hunched and frail in the wheelchair I had trouble believing he was my father. I wheeled him forward but stopped long enough to point at his name chiseled in stone above the entrance. The William P. Rogers Building. "Do you see that, Dad?" He wasn't looking where I was pointing. "Look, above the door."

His eyes rose. He saw his name and smiled weakly.

His colleagues were waiting in the lobby. I wheeled him in and they broke into applause. Dad sprang to life. The color returned to his face. He smiled as he had at countless dinners and press conferences, smiled as he had for countless Tahoe Christmas card pictures. The Rogers smile. He *beamed*. Life regained, if only for a moment.

His colleagues came forward one by one to shake his hand and pat him on the back. He responded with the wide smile and firm grip of a politician running for office.

An hour passed. The nurse and I had decided ahead of time that we wouldn't let him stay more than an hour. When we told Dad it was time to leave, he adamantly refused. "I'm having a great time."

"We think it's best."

"You go, I'm not leaving."

"You don't want to get overly tired."

"Damn it, don't tell me what I want."

We pried him away an hour later.

CHAPTER TWENTY-SEVEN

The Norfolk Historical Society Museum

JEFF AND I drove for an hour before we reached the Adirondacks. It was May 2010, nine years after Dad died, and we were on our way to Norfolk, New York, the town where he was born.

The older Jeff and I get, the more alike we look. Both of us are bald and wear glasses, he has a trim, outdoorsy beard. We took my car, which was the same as his except mine is a pure, unsullied gray, his gray has a faint blue tint. A factory defect, I claimed.

Neither of us had driven through the Adirondacks before.

"I'm surprised," I told him. "It's your kind of country."

"Too far away." Jeff still lived in Oregon. He and his wife were avid bike riders, in addition to being kayakers and canoeists. "We'll get here someday."

"When was the last time you saw Norfolk?"

"Gosh, I think I was a teenager. I remember so little about it."

"Same here. Dad took me one time when I was very young. I vaguely remember a house, which I assume was the house he grew up in, but the picture in my mind is un-captioned, so I can't be sure."

Neither Jeff nor I is a talker. We're both comfortable with silences. I had wondered how much we'd have to say to each other on this trip, but it turned out to be a lot. After we were underway, you couldn't shut us up.

Dad died of congestive heart failure on January 2, 2001, three weeks after the dedication ceremony. He died in the hospital, surrounded by family. He struggled to breathe at the end, which was painful to watch. After his personal effects were packed for us to take home, I went back to check the room to see if we had left anything behind. On the floor beneath his bed, I found his comb, the comb I had used to comb his hair on the way to the dedication. I didn't tell my siblings what I had found, I wanted it for myself. I keep it in my bedroom drawer.

When my siblings and I told Mother that Dad had died, she gave no response, and we couldn't tell if she understood. She died five months later. She was eighty-nine. She stopped eating and drinking, and died a week later on May 27. Her long decline had ended. We briefly debated feeding her intravenously but rejected the idea. She had made up her mind to go. She died in her own bed, surrounded by family. The hospice nurse said it is not uncommon for spouses to die within six months of each other.

"I'll drive anytime you want," Jeff said breaking the silence.

"Thanks. I'm fine."

"You being so much older than me, you might tire."

"I'll let you know. Explain to me again why the hell you booked us at a bed and breakfast?"

"My thinking was that the proprietor would know the town and could connect us with people who knew Dad."

"Are we sharing a room?"

"I booked two rooms."

"Thank God for that at least."

"We do have to share a bathroom."

"Yikes, as you would say."

Jeff looked startled. "I say 'yikes'?"

"You say it all the time. You didn't know?"

"I don't believe you. You're making that up."

"Self-knowledge is somewhat lacking, I see."

The mountains were magnificent. I had seen them from a distance many times as I drove from our Vermont house to Glens Falls, New

York. Their outline stretches north-south with no apparent end, the Great Wall of the North Country. (I have a photo of Dad standing on the Great Wall of China with Nixon. Our son Sam has the coat Dad wore in the picture.)

"One thing I have never been able to understand is how we turned out so differently," Jeff said. "You're indoors, I'm outdoors."

"No clue. The way Mother and Dad's genes combined, I assume. It can't be our upbringing."

"Birth order, maybe?"

"That doesn't ring true," I said.

"You're probably right, but you felt more pressure than I."

"You mean from Dad?"

"Correct. You bore the brunt."

"I thought Dale did."

"No, you. You were the first son."

"Okay, but how does that explain the indoors, outdoors thing?"

"It doesn't. I was changing the subject."

"That does it. You drive."

I pulled over at rest stop. A sign pointed the way to sites within the park.

Jeff got in the drivers side and adjusted the seat. He's an inch shorter than me, and I never let him forget it. "You know, you can raise the seat if you can't see out the windshield. We can buy a booster seat if worst comes to worst."

He adjusted the rearview mirror. "It's going to be a real letdown to drive a dull gray car."

He pulled out of the rest area. There was little traffic on the winding road. The mountain walls funneled us forward.

"Another difference between us is that you served in Vietnam and I didn't."

"You protested in the Moratorium, if I remember correctly."

"I did. It was painful, but I was never in danger."

"Our hospital ship was in Da Nang Harbor or off the coast near the DMZ during my year of combat duty. I spent a number of weeks at bases that were being shelled, both that year and the next when I returned to do a study of Vietnamization for the Pentagon, but I felt guilty when I saw the wounded being helicoptered to our ship for treatment every day. Compared to them I was relatively safe."

"I felt guilty about not serving." I told him about receiving notice I would be inducted in three weeks, and about deciding not to flee to Canada. "I'd sign up but refuse duty in Vietnam. I don't know if I would've had the guts."

"I didn't know that."

"I was so totally self-absorbed in that era I didn't share much with anybody."

"I know a thing or two about self-absorption. You remember when I came to D.C. to tell Mother and Dad I was joining the Navy? Think back to how little I shared with you. The bare minimum."

"What were we afraid of?" I asked.

"I don't know, that we weren't good enough in some undefined way?"

"I think that's it. I know I compared myself to Dad. I didn't have it in me to compete with him. And when I tried —you remember our dinnertime debates?—I'd say to my teenage-self, 'Schmuck, you're arguing politics with the attorney general of the United States.'"

"That didn't stop you. You two argued *all* the time."

"I'm stubborn."

"For me it wasn't Dad," Jeff said. "I did well enough at the things he cared about that he left me alone."

"He did more than leave you alone, he applauded you. Didn't he come to all your football games? Never to mine."

"Okay. What I was trying to say was, he didn't beat up on me like he did you. I wasn't afraid of Dad, I was afraid I wasn't as good as my record. It wasn't until I dropped out of medical school and gradually discovered how I wanted to live my life that I felt self-confident."

"For me, it was quitting the law firm and moving to Paris."

"I admired your guts, I remember."

"Thanks, but it could also be viewed as copping out."

Jeff thought for a moment. "Why are we four so hard on ourselves?

We need to learn how to brag. Dad was a master at stealth bragging."

"We lack his charm."

"Speak for yourself." Before Jeff retired from his legal career, he had earned a master's degree in counseling and now spent his time, when he wasn't kayaking or canoeing, counseling returning veterans from Afghanistan and Iraq. "We were lucky. Dad could be a tough customer at times, but he and Mother gave us love and good values. Look how we turned out. Except for you, we turned out pretty well." He glanced to see if I would react. When I didn't take the bait, he smiled.

Mountain scenery gave way to small towns. We were two hundred miles from New York City and forty miles from the St. Lawrence Seaway and Canada. Until we got to Potsdam, the towns were specks. Potsdam thrust us back into civilization, if only for the few minutes it took to drive through. A college town, it had the bustle of most college towns. And then we were back in relative isolation. We were nineteen miles from the border. We passed through the Village of Norwood and came to the Hamlet of Norfolk.

"Stop," I said. "Pull over."

Jeff pulled to a stop on the shoulder, kicking up dust. "What's wrong?"

A blue sign on a rusted pole stood by the side of the road. We got out and approached the sign.

BIRTHPLACE OF
WILLIAM P. ROGERS
U.S. ATTORNEY GENERAL
1957-1961
U.S. SECRETARY OF STATE
1969-1973

Jeff whipped out his camera and took pictures. Many, many pictures. Jeff does not know when to stop.

Closer to town, another sign welcomed us to Norfolk—"Tops In Towns."

Downtown Norfolk consists of one and a half sparsely populated

Tony and Jeff, Norfolk, New York, 2010

streets. A few stores on the road from Potsdam to Canada, and a few on a cross street, among them an auto parts store, a sports cards store, an ice cream parlor, and a church. The wood frame buildings look no sturdier than wrapping paper. A hollowed-out Easter egg shell of a town.

We found the bed-and-breakfast on a side street. It was close to downtown but was surrounded by empty, rolling land. A pleasant woman greeted us and soon had us connected to the son of Dad's stepbrother, who runs the insurance agency started by Dad's father, Harrison Rogers.

It was late afternoon, and Russell was leaving town at six, but if we got to the insurance agency before then, he would be glad to see us.

The insurance agency was a small wooden house beside the road from Potsdam to Canada with a sign that still said, "The Harrison A. Rogers Insurance Agency."

Russell couldn't have been nicer. He ushered us into the small office and showed us framed photos of Harrison Rogers and Dad, among others, on the wall.

"He was a forceful man," Russell said of his step-grandfather. Russell was the grandson of Harrison's second wife, the woman Harrison married after Dad's mother died. "I was afraid to be in the same room with him. We all tread lightly. Let's take a drive. I'll show you where your father was born and where his parents are buried."

"Won't you be late?" Jeff asked.

Russell checked his watch. "I'll be a little late, but it's okay."

We didn't have far to go. The house where Dad was born was a few blocks away, half a block off the main street. A compact wood frame that had fought a few rounds with the weather, it had an enclosed porch that the present owners said they had added. "It wasn't there when your dad was born." The owners were an elderly couple who had lived there for decades. "I remember when your dad came for the opening of the St. Lawrence Seaway. That was back in...." He turned to his wife, a stooped woman who had the indomitable look of some frail people. "When was it? Do you remember?"

"1959," his wife said.

"Yes, that's it." He swept his hand down to the end of the street, which was two houses away. "There was a farm at the end of the road then. Your dad sat on the porch with us while his security men searched the fields. Made us laugh. The fields have never attacked anyone, far as we know." He pointed to a house directly across the street. "Your dad moved there when he was little." The house was a variation on the theme of Dad's birth house. Fresher paint, slightly bigger.

I tried to imagine what it was like on this street in 1913. My guess, and it was strictly a guess, is that the atmosphere here in town was not dramatically different in the early 20th century than in the early 21st century. This was Lake Wobegon, New York, a town that time forgot.

We thanked the couple and drove the short distance to the cemetery. The graves were in a narrow plot along the side of the road, backed by a line of trees. The kind of country cemetery one drives past without noticing. We got out and stepped onto wet ground. Across the road, fields of tall grass.

Russell led us to the Rogers family plot. Buried there are Dad's father and beloved mother, Myra. Dad's stepmother is not. We asked Russell why. She preferred to be buried at the cemetery where her parents are buried, he explained.

Two small gravestones near Myra and Harrison's have almost been swallowed by the earth. The gravestones of Dad's two brothers, each of whom lived less than a year. One died before Dad was born, the other when Dad was four. We had known about the first brother, but not the second. How painful it must have been for Dad to lose his brothers and his mother.

I couldn't help but contrast this simple country cemetery with Arlington National Cemetery, where Mother and Dad are buried. What a long journey Dad had taken. He was buried on a bitter cold day with full military honors. The notes of a trumpet playing taps cut through the cold. The flag covering Dad's casket was folded and handed to my seated mother who softly but clearly replied, "Thank you very much," the first words she had uttered in a year.

Russell let us stand there as long as we wanted, then drove us back to our car. We shook his hand and thanked him profusely.

NATIVE SON'S SONS RETURN - Two sons of former Secretary of State, William P. Rogers, a Norfolk native, were recently in town and visited their father's birthplace, Bixby Cemetery, where their grandparents, Harrison A. and Myra Rogers are buried, and the Norfolk Museum, where there are many items pertaining to Sec. Rogers. Jeff and Anthony Rogers, from Portland, Oregon and Vermont, stand with Norfolk Town Historian Leon Burnap.

Jeff and Tony with Leon Burnap, town historian of Norfolk, New York
From *NorthCountryNow*, June 17, 2010

"Wow," Jeff said, when we got in the car.

"Too much emotion for one day," I said.

We got something to eat at a generic restaurant along the road to Potsdam, burned out from the emotion and the day's long drive. The next morning we discovered that at this bed-and-breakfast you ate with the owners. The four of us crowded around the small kitchen table and chatted while we ate. The breakfast was excellent, but I am incapable of conversation first thing in the morning. Jeff is no more outgoing than I as a rule, but he can fake it better, and he gave me knowing looks across the table as the proprietor asked me what Nixon was really like. Jeff told me later that I had handled the question well. "What did I say?" "That he was the same in private as he was in public."

The proprietor was also the assistant pastor at one of the town church-es, and she inserted a little religious training before breakfast ended but leavened it with news that she had contacted the town historian on our behalf. "Leon's going to open the Historical Society Museum for you this morning. Normally it doesn't open until noon, but I told him you were driving back to Vermont this afternoon."

"That's very kind of him. And of you," I said, trying to make up for my less than charitable thoughts about early morning chumminess.

We had seen the Norfolk Historical Society Museum on our initial drive through town, in a storefront next to the sports card trading store. Leon would meet us there at 9. We were a little early and parked in front. One advantage of small towns is there's never a parking problem (although residents would probably disagree). A small sign on the door of the museum said "Open Tuesdays and Thursdays from noon to 5."

Leon had been the town historian for two decades and, at one time or another, had served in just about every position the town had to offer. A man of few words, he ushered us into the museum, and by the time he closed the door behind us, I trusted him completely. The museum consists of two cluttered rooms. Letters, photographs, flags, old clocks, on shelves, in cabinets, on tables. A yard sale waiting to happen. Time had not forgotten the town after all, it had just taken up residence in the museum.

From the archives in the front room, Leon pulled out letter after letter, photo after photo, of Dad's childhood and career. An amazing amount of stuff. The family had donated most of Dad's papers to the Cornell Law Library and the State Department, but historians will need to come to Norfolk to get the full picture. Too much to absorb in one morning. Here's where Jeff's photo-taking compulsion was useful, not annoying. When Jeff had worn out his shutter finger documenting what we were seeing, Leon took us into the back room and showed us a card table in the middle of the clutter. On it were memorabilia from Dad's life. "WILLIAM P. ROGERS, NORFOLK'S NATIVE SON," said a sign above the table.

It was startling to see articles about Dad from local newspapers (he got great press in Norfolk), report cards and class photos from his grade school, wedding pictures of Dad's parents, pictures of Dad in his Naval uniform and of Dad with Nixon, on a card table in this unassuming museum. It was even more startling to see a selection of our family Christmas cards, fake smiles and all, spread out on the table. On display were Dale, Jeff, Doug, me, our spouses and children, and, of course, always sitting in the front row, Mother and Dad. In one of the cards Dad is wearing his bright yellow sports jacket. In another, I am. It looked better on you than me, Dad.

AUTHOR'S POSTSCRIPT

A lifetime of thanks to my sister, Dale Rogers Marshall, and my brothers, Jeff and Doug Rogers.

Thirty-nine years of thanks to my wife, Tamara Elliott Rogers.

An essay adapted from this memoir appeared in the Autumn 2015 issue of *The Gettysburg Review*.

Tony Rogers holds degrees from Yale and Harvard Law School. Once upon a time, he was a professional musician, briefly a Wall Street lawyer and for twenty-five years a hospital administrator. He is the winner of the Nilsen Prize for a First Novel and the Writer's Voice Capricorn Prize for a collection of short stories. The Nilsen Prize winning novel, *The Execution of Richard Sturgis, As Told by His Son, Colin*, was published by Southeast Missouri State University Press in 2013. His fiction and non-fiction have appeared in *The Gettysburg Review, Pleiades, Thema, North Dakota Quarterly, Worcester Review*, the *Boston Globe Magazine*, and many others. Rogers lives in Cambridge with his wife Tamara.

Visit www.tonyrogersauthor.com for more information.